Dear Tammy,
Welcome to the Liberty Division!

Cam

A Moral Case *for*
CAPITALISM

Why Basic Human Morality Calls for Free Markets

CAMERON KAWATO

EDITED BY
ADAM ROSEN

Copyright © 2017 - Cameron Kawato

A Moral Case *for*
CAPITALISM

Why Basic Human Morality Calls for Free Markets

CONTENTS

Foreword *by Lee Bailiff*..................... xi

Introduction................................ 1

THE CASE

1. Wages: Why the Difference?.............. 14
2. Capitalism is Anti-Sexist and Anti-Racist .. 33
3. Regulations, Mandates, and Those Darned Monopolies............................. 41
4. Capitalism Satisfies Demand—Communism Brings Starvation........... 52
5. Taxes and Government Spending 57
6. Technological Advancements Bring Big Rewards for All................ 67

7. Health Care: The Dreaded Topic 77

8. Free Trade Makes Both Sides Better Off .. 88

9. Are We Destroying the Environment? 96

10. Profits Are Not Evil. 104

11. Coercion vs. Liberty. 110

12. Independence, Personal Responsibility, and the Welfare State 122

13. Self-Enhancement. 131

14. Venezuela and the Tale of Two Koreas .. 137

15. The Need for the Right Culture 143

16. A Christian Perspective 150

17. Final Notes 155

Endnotes 163

DEDICATED TO

*The United States of America.
I love you from sea to shining sea.*

FOREWORD

by LEE BAILIFF

I've been teaching economic principles at the collegiate level since 2006. Thousands of individual students have entered my classroom since my first semester. Some of these students, naturally, performed much better than others. The key to an outstanding grade in my class has never been entirely due to natural aptitude (although that doesn't hurt). The key has been, and remains, simply doing the work.

Cameron does the work.

I enjoy most those students I never have to worry about. They show up. They read their assignments. They ask questions when they don't understand the material. They study. They work. The wage for their labor is not only the ultimate grade on their transcript. The wage is also the knowledge gained and, to a far greater extent, the practice of using their minds to critically analyze problems, develop solutions, and defend those solutions.

I've never taught a stupid student. But, I've taught countless lazy ones. Students that won't just not do the work – but, don't want to think. Because, it's easier to just latch on to what someone else has already thought.

Cameron doesn't do that. I think this book is sufficient proof.

At the end of each semester I want my students to fully understand how much I expect each and every one of them to take their minds seriously. To be where the proverbial buck stops. To take responsibility for their world view and accept that they are just as responsible for defending that view as those who disagree with them are responsible for defending theirs.

This requires diligence, patience, conviction, commitment, and the ability to communicate effectively.

Cameron does this. Again, I think this book is sufficient proof.

I welcome you to read this work. If you come across a section that upsets you, I challenge you to analyze the specific reasons why it does so. I challenge you to defend the position you believe that section is attacking. And, I challenge you to be open to the possibility that you need to change your mind.

There's nothing shameful about changing one's mind. It is, after all, the only reasonable reaction to receiving a better argument built upon better information than we possessed before.

I sincerely believe it is better to gain a more

FOREWORD

correct view of reality than it is to win an argument.

Writing this book was Cameron's effort to gain a more correct view of reality. Read it with the same goal.

And, once you've finished, if you are convinced nothing has changed within your mind, I only ask that you do the work that result requires you to do.

Your mind is a wonderful tool. Use it. Even when it exhausts you (as it will). In fact, relish that exhaustion. It is similar to the anxious high associated with love, and the nervous sweat associated with courage. All are major reasons life is worth living.

Do the work. And, enjoy doing it.

INTRODUCTION

Dear reader,

We are about to reach a turning point in American history. The ideological war between limited government and big government is beginning to heat up hotter than it has in recent memory, and we will have to decide as a society which side we will take. This is not a question of turning right or left; it is a question of going up or down. Will we sink to the depths of Soviet gulags and shortages? Or will we rise, like we have before, to the heights of personal liberty and responsibility?

Even though millions upon millions of people have died under communist and socialist regimes in the twentieth century alone, the two ideologies still win hearts and minds to this day.[1] This is because they appear to offer the perfect plan. What person in their right mind would not want to live in a world where everyone was taken care of and there were no worries over things like food, shelter, clothing, or personal security? A quick look through history, however, clearly shows that these are not the outcomes that communism and socialism achieve. Time and time again, the two ideologies have starved, overworked, and brought death to the citizens living under their yoke.

It is not as though there are two competing sides in this debate, where one side has all of the ideas for creating a real utopia and the other side does not want this utopia. Utopia seems great—in theory. However, in the real world, there are reasons for opposing big government. And, as history has shown, there are very real reasons to fear the expansion of government.

Though communism and socialism are technically two different political ideologies, they share one crucial aspect: they both restrict free markets. This lack of liberty in the marketplace leads to a lack of liberty on the individual level. Joseph Stalin was a communist. He slaughtered millions of his own people, and the vast majority of those who survived his brutality did not receive the utopia they were promised—or anything close to it. Soviet citizens were promised an ample supply for basic needs like food, water, and shelter, but were given only shortages. If socialism and communism were such loving and compassionate ideologies, why would they lead to these kinds of outcomes?

The truth is that when it comes to economic systems that improve people's lives, capitalism has the upper hand, by leaps and bounds. This is why I wrote

INTRODUCTION

this book. There is a rock-solid case for capitalism on moral grounds, and this perspective is rarely discussed in public discourse. I will attempt to make this case to you in as few words as possible, while showing you why I believe big-government ideologies are actually immoral.

That being said, I also wrote this book with the modern conservative and libertarian in mind. Its goal is to act as a sort of handbook aimed at teaching people who already believe in the free market how to argue for their stances. Along with those people, it was written for those who, in my opinion, have been deceived their entire lives. They have been deceived by academia, Hollywood, the mainstream media, and other powerful institutions equally hostile to free-market capitalism. They have been told that capitalism is evil, greedy, and only feeds the rich by hurting the poor. In reality, the opposite is true. Big government feeds the elites while keeping the populace in the dirt.

My intention was to make this book digestible to anyone. There's a joke that economists take one of the simplest fields of study and attempt to make it as difficult to understand as possible. You will not find that approach here. You do not need to be a Harvard economist to understand my arguments, and there is only one (simple) math equation. Also, the chapters are written to be short and to the point. In other words, I attempted to save you from as much fat as possible. If this book were a steak, it would be a sirloin tip, because most people just do not have time to read a huge manuscript in order to learn something that could have been summarized in a few pages.

The inspiration for writing this book came from a single conversation I had with a friend. She mentioned that in a class earlier that day, she had participated in a debate over whether or not profits and wage differences were a bad thing, and she wanted advice on what to say. More specifically, the debate was over whether or not it was right for the owner of a huge company to make millions of dollars while a common worker at the company makes minimum wage. She was on the side of the free market while her opposition was on the side opposed to the free market. Her opponent's reasoning went like this: one person was taking home truckloads of cash while many people under them were struggling to survive, which is therefore unjust and unfair. When an argument is presented in these emotional terms, it can be difficult to mount a challenge. Accordingly, this book will teach you how to argue for free markets using the same language as those who despise it. That is, the language of emotion.

In my view, the Left uses the language of emotion and feelings while the Right uses the language of logic, reason, and numbers. For example, a politician may come out and say that if we lower taxes to a certain percent, it would create hundreds of thousands of new jobs. Sounds nice, but all it would take to halt this change is for an opposing politician to come out and say that we need to provide more for

INTRODUCTION

the single mother of three. She is suffering, and the other politician's proposed tax code change will only cause her more suffering. This is enough to make the average, good-hearted person turn to the second politician's plan. You can see how the two arguments are different in presentation as well as substance.

Humans are more receptive to emotional anecdotes than logical figures. I think this is neither good nor a bad. For example, a football coach whose team is losing does not waltz into the locker room during the halftime break and say, "Yeah, we have a 32 percent chance of coming back based on statistics. 32 percent may not be a lot, but it's more than zero. Now get out there and win." Instead, he taps into the emotions of the players to get them pumped up for the second half in order to win. He gives them stories of teams that have come back from the brink of defeat, and makes his players believe they can win.

This natural tendency to appeal to emotion tends to be exploited by those on the Left more than those on the Right. The debate over wages is a good example of this. Many CEOs of huge companies make tremendous amounts of money every year while those lower on the ladder make considerably less. It's very easy to point to that and say it is unfair or unjust. When Senator Bernie Sanders says that the richest people in our country need to "pay their fair share," it sounds like those people have cheated the rest of the population by not paying enough in taxes. This suggestion is enough to inflame anyone, but the point is that it was an appeal to emotion by telling people that they have basically been cheated.

Running for office or advocating for your cause is obviously much different than running a football team, but you can see how the use of emotion can influence people. This is most easily displayed in speeches delivered by Presidents Reagan and Nixon. Reagan not only had charm, but he spoke to the heart rather than the mind, while Nixon spoke to the mind alone. There is a reason Reagan is called the Great Communicator.

To be clear, I do not believe that speaking to the heart or emotions is necessarily a bad thing. Our emotions are what make us human rather than just another mammal. My point is that when one side uses emotion to take advantage of the audience while the other side does not, a lopsided debate will result. Accordingly, the following chapters will show you how to tap into emotion to make a counterargument. Whether you already agree with me that the free market is the best route for humanity or not, I hope I offer you some new insight into this debate, because it is a very serious debate.

I spent several years in Texas away from California where I grew up. During this time, I saw something that I never saw in California: "Help wanted" signs. This was a shock to me coming from a state where the number one complaint was that it was "impossible to find a job." These signs were in the windows of Texas small businesses and franchise businesses alike,

INTRODUCTION

and were something that I had (ironically) only really seen in Hollywood movies before. How could the two biggest states in the country be in such different situations? One had freer markets while the other would not shock anyone if it decided to become a purely communist state tomorrow.

It is my belief that within twenty years or so, political debate in America will no longer be between Republicans and Democrats, or even conservatives and liberals—it will be between libertarians and tyrants. For evidence of this growing divide, you don't have to look much further than our universities, which are producing people who think it's okay to meet a different opinion with threats—or use—of force. The rise in popularity of the Antifa (or "anti-fascist") movement is very telling, because it reflects the values of many young people today (at least, those in college). In their view, speech they do not agree with is hate speech, and thus they have the right to forcibly stop people whose opinions they oppose from speaking.

In a perfect world, we would come to policy decisions based on tangible evidence rather than emotion. However, we cannot sit here and just logically argue our way to defeat. The stakes are simply too high and the human race depends on our success.

The bullying tactics of many on the Left must be met with a response that speaks their own language.

For example, when a big-government advocate attacks a limited-government supporter for supposedly not caring about the poor and only caring about the rich, the person supporting limited government tends to become defensive. They will say the depiction of them just isn't true, and that they *do* actually care about the poor but have different opinions on how to ultimately help them. While this is true, it is only half of the story. *Very rarely* will you see the advocate of limited government point out the fact that it is actually big government that hurts the poor. It is actually *those* policies that keep the poor poor and the rich rich while applying huge amounts of pressure on the middle class, effectively pushing them down into poverty. Big government needs poor people. It needs them because with a healthy middle class, there will be less of a desire for those big-government policies. It tells poor people that only *it* can take care of them, that they are being oppressed by evil capitalists. In reality, these "evil capitalists" just want to leave you to live your life and create an environment where anyone can rise.

Think of debating like a sword duel. If you are facing an opponent with a sword, you can only block your opponent's attacks for so long. Eventually, one of their strikes will land, or you will become too fatigued to defend yourself any longer and will never be able to launch any of your own strikes. In

INTRODUCTION

our example, the small-government advocate who claims that it's untrue that they don't care about the poor is only blocking; they never strike. This book will teach you how to strike as well, because while defense is important, you cannot win without an offense. And, as critical examination makes clear, the truth is that those who advocate for big government have no defense. They cannot call upon history, logic, or the economic statistics of countries living under huge governments in order to show that they are right, because all of these things point toward small government being the best option. Even places like the Nordic states, which have become the poster child for successful societies for many on the American Left, are turning back toward the free market because of this reality.[2]

You already hold the economic facts and history. You can point to nations like Venezuela, Cuba, North Korea, and the Soviet Union, places where people suffered horribly—and continue to suffer—because of big government's (mis)rule. Soon you, too, will wield the sword of emotion, which cuts much more deeply than logic, for reasons explained above. However, we should only use this tactic when it is deployed against us. It takes fire to fight fire.

Another important way the Left appeals to emotion is through identity politics. Many of their leaders divvy us up according to race, gender, sexual orientation, or socioeconomic status. Capitalism is for all. It does not discriminate and it does not play identity politics. Modern libertarians and conservatives want to unite the entire country under the shield of liberty, instead of pitting different groups against each other for votes.

In the conservative community, it is well known and widely talked about that American liberalism runs our culture. It runs academia, where students are given "safe spaces" when their preferred candidate does not win an election, and where they learn that facts are subjective, and that white folks have oppressed the entire world and continue to do so to this day. It runs Hollywood and the TV industry, which constantly tell us that humanity is destroying the earth, and that flyover states are backward places full of gunslinging bandits. It runs the mainstream media, where Former President Obama is exalted like a god among men, and any conservative politician is attacked on all fronts because there is an "R" next to their name.

As a result, our national divide grows wider and wider, and Lincoln's warning grows ever more relevant. Lincoln believed that if America fell, it would not fall from the outside, but from within. It is important to point out that this is not a partisan issue; there are plenty of Democrats who understand and accept the value of the free market, just as there are plenty of Republicans, especially in Congress, who seem to reject basic free-market policies with their votes.

I believe that if we are to take back the culture, the best place to start is on the outside. The walls

INTRODUCTION

of our culture-creating centers are simply too high and too thick to take from the inside. A young, well-meaning conservative will be chewed up and spit out in Hollywood. We must lay siege by simply exposing the truths of big government. People are smart, and they will be able to recognize that they have been bamboozled by these institutions. After this is done, the indoctrination institutions of liberal culture will fall on their own.

My point is this: when thousands of young American men landed at Normandy, they did not turn their backs, reboard their landings crafts, and hightail it home because they realized that they had just entered Hell on Earth. They had a decision to make. They could have fled and lived for tyranny, or fought and died for liberty. They chose to die for liberty, and today we live in a much freer world because of them. Let us make the same courageous decision. Let us not stand by and live for tyranny. Let us stand *firm* and fight for liberty.

THE CASE

1. WAGES: WHY THE DIFFERENCE?

Some try to argue that the difference in pay between jobs is immoral. They claim that if Person A makes more money than Person B in a given year, Person A probably stepped on Person B in some way or committed some other immoral act in order to become wealthier than the next person. They claim that this is unjust and that society must do something about it.

Usually, the prescription for this inequality is redistributing wealth. In other words, spreading the wealth, or taking from some to give to others. The truth is, the fact that one person makes more money than another is not a sign of wrongdoing or inequity in the system as a whole. This *could* be a sign of inequity in some economies, such as pure communist and socialist states where the people are poor and the leaders are filthy rich. The real evil happens when someone tries to forcibly even the scales while claiming that Person A did not earn that wealth justly when they actually did.[3] Wage inequality does not mean that the rich have stolen from the poor in some fashion; it means that the rich have offered a more sought-after product, service, or idea, and have traded that product, service, or idea more often or for a higher value than someone with less wealth has traded theirs.

Before we continue, we should think about what a wage actually is. At its core, a wage is the same thing as a price tag or a bill. When you go to the restaurant for dinner, you are really paying the restaurant a wage for their service (cooking, table service, ensuring that the health code is being followed, etc.). When you hire a painter, you also pay them a wage in exchange for their service. When you buy toothpaste in the store, you are paying a wage to cover all the costs of producing, transporting, and stocking the item. The same is true when you hire an employee. When a restaurant owner pays their cook, they are paying for the cooking service, just as the customer is paying for the restaurant service.

This is why we see varying wages across positions and industries. You would be appalled if you were charged $60 for a single meal at a fast food restaurant, but it would not be such a surprise at the nicest restaurant in the city. The same is true for workers. Each is paid according to his or her price of labor. This rule of paying someone what his or her work is worth is something that can only be violated in a state-run economy, which is something we will go over soon.

If you are hired for a job and offer the company sixty dollars' worth of labor per hour, they will offer you sixty dollars per hour for that job. If, however, they offer something like forty dollars per hour and you still accept the job, you will no longer provide sixty dollars' worth of labor each hour. You will give them forty dollars' worth of labor per hour, because you can get away with it, since that is their compensation rate—and they have no real way to force you to put in sixty dollars' worth of labor each hour if they are only giving you forty dollars an hour. If they try to extract more value from your labor—perhaps by threats, or a hostile work environment—you can always quit. By thinking about wages in this way, we can see that it is a two-way street. Businesses have incentive to offer you a fair wage; otherwise, you will stop showing up to work.

But what if a company with jobs that require sixty dollars' worth of labor per hour attempts to hire employees for only forty dollars per hour? Even if the company could convince some people to take the job, how will it mine that extra twenty dollars of value out of the employees every hour? After all, they will work according to their level of payment, like you did in the previous example. In America, there is no way to force someone to work for more than what they are being paid. That would require coercion, which is illegal.

WAGES: WHY THE DIFFERENCE?

Economics can easily become emotional. It is understandable that people would respond positively to a minimum wage policy that would pay more to the busboy at the local restaurant. I am sure he is a nice guy and all, but who is really paying the price for a mandated wage increase? After minimum wage hikes, employers must now decide how to pay this new, higher wage. They could fire some workers, raise prices, stop expanding/creating new jobs, or even pay themselves less, in cases where the business is very profitable. But really, should the employer, and all of the people that are hurt by this policy (including coworkers *and* customers), pay for choices and circumstances that were made outside of their realm of influence? That's like putting someone in prison for a crime that was committed by someone else. Thus, the clarifying question to ask is: should someone pay for the decisions someone else made?

Cleaning tables at a restaurant will admittedly not make someone a millionaire overnight and, in some cities and areas, this wage might be extremely difficult to live off of. My point is that it is not the business owner's responsibility to make the busboy comfortable. Let's even say that this is the best busboy in the country; there never seems to be a dirty table when a new party walks in the door. Because he is offering a highly sought-after skill in the eyes of many restaurant owners, if his current boss is not paying him fairly, someone else eventually will.

A MORAL CASE FOR CAPITALISM

At the end of the day, when you forcibly change the outcomes of a free market, someone is inevitably going to be hurt. It will never be a win-win situation, as someone is going to have to be on the losing end of the stick. This is because redistributing wealth does not create more wealth, it just moves around the wealth that was already created before. A politician who says they are going to grow the economy by essentially redistributing wealth is comically inaccurate and misguided. This is because someone will be forced to give up money that they worked for so that it can go to someone else who did not earn as much. No new wealth will be created, and the economy will only be slowed, because now both sides have less incentive to create. The wealthy person has less incentive to create because that new creation is just going to be taxed or simply taken away, while the less wealthy person has less incentive to create, because they are expecting a subsidy from the government.

Some also argue that the United States should raise the minimum wage because "evil" corporations and bosses are stealing from their employees by exploiting their labor. They claim again that some sort of injustice has occurred because the leaders are paid more while workers are paid less. In reality, the employers are exploiting their workers' labor while the workers are exploiting their employers' capital. Each has something the other does not have, but wants. The business owner wants manpower and the workers want money, so they trade for these assets.

WAGES: WHY THE DIFFERENCE?

In reality, the free market is completely moral when the rules of law are followed. It's when the government steps in and steals from people that we stumble into immoral grounds. The free market will always provide payment that is fair and just; only an economy riddled with government regulations and rules will sustain an economy that pays people too little for long. Any competent businessperson wants the best employees, and the only way to get the best employees is to pay them fairly. Paying anything less than a fair wage will open the window for another business to poach that employee by offering them a higher wage. The free market is constantly checking itself to ensure that people are being paid the right price. This is one of the most fundamental aspects of the "invisible hand" identified by Adam Smith. At any moment, another business can offer a particular worker a better incentive.

This is not to say that if someone is underpaid they will instantly be offered a higher paycheck, but it is the case that big companies and small businesses alike are searching for these employees in order to take them from other companies to remain competitive. Major league sports offer a simple example. Teams compete during the offseason to sign the best players. To do this, they need to offer incentives based on a player's performance. It isn't considered wrong or immoral for a second-string lineman to secure a smaller contract than an all-star quarterback.

Raising the minimum wage would put everyone

who produces less than the wage pays out of a job. This is a win-win for big-government advocates: they get the votes from both the people who the businesses were able to keep employed and now receive a bigger check and from the people the businesses had to fire, who now rely on the state for welfare and other subsidies. "Big government" is constantly stripping people of their independence in this way. Every economic policy it enacts brings more and more people down into the ground, forcing them into submission to the state.

We have no way of knowing if this result is intentional or not, but the inevitable consequence will be as I just described. One metaphor to think of is wildfires. Nearly every year, my home state of California experiences very devastating wildfires. These big conflagrations arise because we stop the small, natural ones which, if left untouched, would clear out all of the underbrush but keep the trees safe. However, when we stop this natural process from happening, the underbrush grows until the next wildfire can reach the canopy of the forest and cause massive destruction. Likewise, when government gets involved and attempts to force the market to act in a certain (unnatural) way, it ends up burning all of us.

Big-government political parties rely on people's failures. If there were enough ladders in the economy for people to climb, there would be no need for big-government policies, so these policies end up creating an economy that is dependent upon big government. They know that if people were able to live on their own and provide for themselves, nobody would feel the need to vote for politicians whose "solutions" come in the form of more government. They know that if people of different races, genders, and/or orientations did not feel like victims, there would be no need for their party. Thus, it is in the best interest of these political parties to keep as many people poor, desperate, and victimized as possible while blaming their condition on capitalists.

In a free market, every ladder is open. Anyone can achieve any dream they want. Of course, some people are born into much easier situations, but they cannot be blamed for that, especially since their parents or grandparents probably worked very hard in order to give them the comfort they enjoy. There is no law that bars anyone from achieving a certain position in life, except for the few statutes that keep people below a certain age from running for certain public offices.

Raising the minimum wage bars the teenager who dreams of owning their own restaurant someday from working at one and gaining the experience they need to open their own. Minimum wage laws tell everyone that cannot yet produce more than the value of the minimum wage that they cannot compete. This is, of course, not true at all, but when businesses are forced to pay a certain price for labor, there will be some people who cannot reach that bar.

Sometimes the best way to reach the top of a particular industry is to start at the bottom. Someone who dreams of starting their own car company would probably benefit from working in a Chevrolet assembly plant. However, if the company cannot hire this person because of a minimum wage law, that person will be forced to miss out on a potentially valuable opportunity.

Minimum wage doesn't only hurt workers. An increase in prices also occurs when wages are artificially raised, hurting consumers.[4] This results in higher costs for everyone, *including* those who had their wages raised. The cost of artificially raised wages has to be made up somehow; somebody has to pay the price. But these price changes are hardly noticed, because they are usually spread out over a long period of time. Eventually, however, people begin blaming companies for setting prices that are too high—rather than the politicians whose policies forced the company to raise its prices. This is another example of how sneaky big-government policies can be in hurting people and casting the blame on someone else. Since economic movements are so hard to see and can take some time, these changes can easily be blamed on the free market when in actuality, the market was never entirely free.

When you regulate wages, just like when you regulate any other part of an economy, black markets arise. If minimum wages become too high, we will begin to see workers paid under the table in cash.

WAGES: WHY THE DIFFERENCE?

This means those people are no longer going to pay income tax, and will essentially be freeloading off of every public project. Just like when you ban guns in a city—criminals find a way to get them under the table, while law abiders are left without them. One of the deadliest—and most telling—black markets in America is the illegal drug market. There is still an enormous demand for drugs, even though they are banned (with the exception of marijuana, which is legal in a few states). People still find a way to distribute and consume them.

Thanks to competition, people are paid exactly what they are worth relative to their production in the free market. This is because businesses must compete with each other to stay afloat. Just as businesses compete for customers, it is equally true that businesses compete for the best employees. This means that if someone is being underpaid, or paid less than what their work is worth, another business is will come along and offer them the wage they deserve in order to take advantage of their production and efficiency. If you do not fairly compensate a good worker, they will find a boss who will.

To provide an example, this principle was demonstrated in early 2014, when a startup in Silicon Valley tried to poach a computer engineer from Google. The startup offered the engineer a whopping $500,000 in yearly salary. He declined the offer, however, because he was already being paid roughly three million dollars per year (and probably health plus other benefits) at Google.[5] If Google were committing an injustice against this engineer by paying him, say, $250,000 a year, the young startup would have been there to remedy the injustice by paying him something closer to what he deserved. This holds true for all forms of work, not just computer coding. It would be pure stupidity for an employer to underpay good workers, because if they did, based on the fact that other companies are looking for the workers' skills, the company would not be in business very long.

This phenomenon also occurs at the small business level. If there were an injustice going on and a secretary were getting paid less than what they deserved relative to the value they brought to the business, another business owner would offer that secretary a wage high enough to poach their talent. Neither the best athlete nor the best janitor will ever be out of a job.

Some jobs also command a bigger check because of the difficulty level or demand for the job. Major League Baseball players make millions of dollars each year, while the concession workers at the stadium make considerably less. This is not unfair or unjust. A concession worker does not need to be able to bat .300 consistently; a legendary baseball player is expected to. Also, millions of Americans go to baseball games each year to see these players display their talents. The truth is that the fans are paying to see the players, not the grounds crew, the concession workers, or the janitors. So, there is a higher demand for good baseball players than there is for a good grounds crew, and thus they are paid according to the demand for their services. This is good for everyone, even the concession workers. Baseball talent brings fans to the stadium, and fans in the stadium means hot dogs will be purchased, which means there needs to be someone to sell the hot dogs, which means another job will be created. No baseball players means no stadium, which means no jobs for the concession workers, janitors, or grounds crew.

As discussed above, some people are upset over the fact that CEOs are given such big paychecks while those on the lower end of the ladder are given so little. They argue that all of the money in the economy is being funneled to the rich CEOs even though all they have to do, supposedly, is sit back and accept their payment while they swim in pools filled with liquid gold.

It is true that many CEOs make very pretty pennies from their positions, but the question is, what did they go through to get there and what are their responsibilities compared to their lower-level employees? And is this difference in pay warranted or not?

Steve Easterbrook, the CEO of McDonald's, was given a salary of $15.4 million in 2016 (this includes base wages plus all benefits).[6] This is obviously considerably more than the wages of the cashiers and other low-level employees. However, Easterbrook has a very different job than them. If someone making your burger makes a mistake and puts pickles on it when you asked for none, you get upset and vow to never return to *that* McDonald's before returning three days later for a burger. If Easterbrook makes a mistake, it could cost the company their value. Depending on how bad the mistake is, the company could even go out of business. Nearly two million people would lose their jobs, and hundreds of countries would lose out on a great product. Simply put, there is a lot of weight resting on the shoulders of this CEO, whereas there is very little resting on the shoulders of a cashier at your local fast-food franchise.

Another reason for the pay difference here is the talent required for the job. Any one of us could very likely go to McDonald's and learn how to make their burgers in less than a day. But to learn how to run the entire company would take months or even years of study. Even then, not all of us would be ready for that job. LeBron James is not worth $485 million just because he can flip burgers. I'm sure that he can flip burgers if he wants, but his basketball talent makes him worth much more than his burger-flipping talent.

Let's pretend that McDonald's fires Easterbrook and distributes his yearly salary throughout the company to all employees. Never mind the fact that burger-flipper and cashier are not the only two jobs at McDonald's. They offer plenty of well-paying jobs, so not all roughly 375,000 McDonald's employees are being paid minimum wage.[7] If McDonald's chose to get rid of Easterbrook and distribute his earnings equally, each employee would receive a wage increase of $41.07 per year. Now the employees

WAGES: WHY THE DIFFERENCE?

would all be $41.07 more wealthy, and McDonald's is gone because they no longer have a leader. With it went hundreds of thousands of jobs and a product that makes many people's lives easier. The entire world would be worse off because of it.

Another argument against free-market wages is that employers force employees into low-wage jobs. But actually, nobody is ever paid a wage that they did not agree to voluntarily. Before someone is officially hired there is always paperwork to complete, and in that paperwork is a contract that clearly states the wage. If someone does not want the payment that is being offered, or if they believe they deserve more, they should renegotiate or refuse to sign the contract and find another employer. Nobody can force anyone to do anything in a free market. Only when government officials say that we must forcibly tax those who have done well for themselves does force come into the picture.

Of course, many argue that, for many people, there are simply no other jobs available out there that pay a better wage. For example, people who live in a small town where there are only low-wage jobs or people who do not have the education level or experience to command a higher wage may face this situation. While this issue may arise in some cases, you cannot force a business owner to pay a wage higher than what they can afford or what the job demands because it is not the business owner's responsibility to take care of someone else. It is the business owner's responsibility to run a business. You also cannot blame an employer if someone did not devote themselves to learning skills that would increase their value. In a free market, everyone is personally responsible for themselves. Of course, people will go through hard times. Jobs may be lost or a life crisis may arise. At that point, it is on the community to help lift this person up, as we will explore later.

It is not immoral when a business cannot offer someone more than they produce. What is immoral is forcing someone to pay a wage they do not want to pay, and in some cases, cannot pay. Nobody would force someone to work below a certain wage (or for no payment), because that would clearly be a form of slavery, but for some reason many people think it is warranted to force someone to pay more for a job than it is worth. This is no different than forcing people to pay ten dollars for a loaf of bread because a group of wheat farmers voted for it.

Businesses, just like consumers, have demands for certain services and will always be looking for whoever provides the best service at the cheapest price. Consumers do this as well. Are consumers evil when they try to find the best product or service they can at the best price? No. When consumers do not hire a mechanic that charges more on average and does a worse job on average, they are not evil. The same applies for businesses. They are not evil for seeking the best talent and paying that talent accordingly. This isn't greed; it's common sense. Not

WAGES: WHY THE DIFFERENCE?

to say potential employees should be looked at as "products," but they *are* offering a service, just like the mechanic in our example. It is not evil to pay someone what they deserve, but it *is* evil to force someone to pay more for something than they think is fair. Would you pay a body shop that does a very subpar job $300 to repair your car? Or would you rather pay a different shop that does great work $200 for the same job? Of course you would choose the second option, but by the logic of those who stand against free markets, your choice is morally tainted.

There are plenty of examples of people who became the wealthiest people in the world despite starting out with very little. Thomas Peterffy was a Hungarian immigrant who came to this country speaking little English. He is now worth roughly $13.7 billion. Alec Gores, an Israeli immigrant, came to the United States at the age of fifteen and has worked to establish his worth at roughly $2.1 billion. Oprah Winfrey was born into poverty in Mississippi and is now worth roughly $3 billion.[8] The list goes on. Was it harder for these people to make it than those born into riches or even the middle class? Of course it was. But the fact that there are so many examples of people rising out of the depths of poverty is proof that there is no conspiracy against the poor. All of these people had something to offer and, above all, they never quit. It is immoral to say, as many have said before, "You did not make that" to someone who actually *did* make that. Yes, some people start out in a very comfortable position, with a good family, a good education, and little need to worry about food or clothing when they are young. However, in order to make the argument that the rich are actively keeping the poor down in a vast conspiracy, you would have to not be able to find a single instance where a poor person rose from poverty into the upper 1 percent. I just gave you three of many.

Relatedly, is evil to punish someone because their parents, grandparents, or great-grandparents made good life decisions and thus had a lot to pass down to them. This should be called caring for your children, but, many times, big-government politicians claim it is evil and greedy. Gaining and maintaining wealth takes a certain mindset. There is a reason that we frequently hear stories about people who win millions in the lottery but are then poor again the next year: they did not handle their money appropriately. It is immoral to punish those who have handled their money correctly to try to fix the mistakes of those who have not.

The goal of the free market is not to ensure that everyone is paid the same wage. Instead, the goal of the free market is to ensure that everyone is paid a wage that reflects their value—and it does a very good job at this. The free market rightly forces people to help each other out in an altruistic manner so that they can then help themselves and their families. You must offer something of value to others, whether that be a good, service, or idea in order to feed your family. Socialism, communism, big government—or whatever else you want to call systems of redistribution—are immoral. They force people to give up what they have earned or built in order to give it to someone who did not do the same.

Free-market capitalism is morally upstanding when it comes to wages because it forces employers to pay a fair wage. If they do not, nobody will work for them and they will go out of business. Big government and its brothers create evil policies concerning wages because they try to force people to pay wages that do not match the value of the services the people receiving the wages provide.

QUICK-DRAW POINTS:

- Minimum wage laws wind up hurting the very people they claim to help by putting business owners in situations where their only option is to let go of some of their workers, raise prices for customers, or stop creating new jobs.

- Minimum wage laws suffocate business expansion, which slows economic and job growth.

- Minimum wage laws effectively bar people who cannot yet produce the value of the minimum wage from participating in the labor market.

- Free markets distribute pay based solely upon supply and demand. There is high demand for good workers, which is why the best ones are never out of a job for long.

A MORAL CASE FOR CAPITALISM

- Free markets are free from force or coercion, unlike markets with government regulations, which, in essence, apply force.

- Forcing someone to work for free is undoubtedly wrong. On the flip side, forcing someone to pay an excessive price for labor (or any service) is wrong as well.

2. CAPITALISM IS ANTI-SEXIST AND ANTI-RACIST

Some accuse the free market of directly oppressing, or allowing people to oppress, minority races and the female sex. This is simply untrue. If anything, the free market actually combats things like racism, sexism, homophobia, and other prejudices. This is because the free market doesn't care what color your skin is or what gender you are, and discrimination based on such shallow reasoning is extremely expensive. The free market only cares about cash. This can seem cold, but as we will discuss, it actually makes for a moral society.

Let's assume that a local burger joint chooses to not serve a certain race of people for no reason other than the owner is racist. The first thing that would happen is that the burger joint will miss out on potential profit. Assuming all the employees stay even though this terrible decision was made, the owner is going to take the hit of this lost profit. Once the community catches wind of this vile policy, they will stop eating there because the decision is simply unacceptable to most, if not all, of them. The owner will then not be able to cover the following month's expenses, which will run the company out of business and into the ground.

The example above is an extreme outlier, of course. Of the millions of businesses in the United States, few would ever act in such a way. And if they did, they would not be in business for long. The reality is that business owners do not care about the color of their customers. They care about making payroll, covering expenses, paying the bills, and still being able to feed their families after being suffocated by taxes and government regulations.

One real-life example of this happened in January of 2017, when a Dairy Queen in Illinois had to shut its doors after the owner tossed racial slurs at a customer.[9] The sheer outrage over the incident caused the owner to lose his franchising rights with Dairy Queen, and the store was closed. The government did not have to do anything; the free market solved the problem more quickly and efficiently than the government could have.

Let's pretend that someone purchases a bar. Business is booming, and the investment turns out to be a good risk to have taken. Time passes, and the bar naturally develops into a gay bar, but the owner is homophobic and hates what has happened. They could do a few things. They could ban people they

CAPITALISM IS ANTI-SEXIST AND ANTI-RACIST

don't like from the bar, or they could intentionally give horrible service to them in hopes of driving them away. If the owner bans all gay people from the bar, they will lose all of their income and the bar will fall into the red, ready to be repossessed by the bank. If they drive their unwanted customers off with intentionally bad service, the other patrons, who are good people, will see this injustice and not want to return. The result will be the same: the owner will be run out of business because of their hatred.

Keep in mind that the Jim Crow laws were mandated by government. When water fountains were put in public places, they cost the government more to install simply because there had to be different water pipe routes, more fountains, etc. for different races. Thus, discrimination is very costly. America is one of the most accepting countries in the world, if not *the* most. We live happily among people of all different races from all different countries, backgrounds, and cultures. We can't stand injustice, and if a business were to discriminate against someone based on something superficial, they would not be a business for very much longer.

The same is true when hiring people. To illustrate this, I'll return to sports analogies. When a new quarterback is recruited, do you really think that any team takes skin color into account? No. Coaches couldn't care less if the person were all the colors of the rainbow. What the team cares about is touchdown-to-interception ratios, arm strength and accuracy, and whether or not the player can elude a blitzing defense. The same holds true for businesses. What color your skin may be means nothing. This is true in all businesses, as they compete with each other just as sports teams do. A marketing firm does not care what you look like—they care how well you can market something.

Some claim that capitalism is racist because some races have outperformed others by economic metrics. But if this were true, why does a minority race outperform whites in America? Asians have a higher median income than any other race in America.[10] If the system were truly set up in order to only help whites while hindering others, would we really see this outcome? To quote Ben Shapiro, "This explains why, mysteriously, the Constitution is in Korean."[11]

You will often hear people throwing around the myth that women are paid seventy-seven cents for every dollar a man is paid for the same exact amount of work at the same exact job. They will say this is because we live in a patriarchal society where only men have power, and are thus paid more and have better opportunities. Though this idea has been debunked by several economists, including a female economist at Harvard University, many politicians still tote it around for votes.[12]

The "seventy-seven cents for every dollar" myth does not account for life choices made by men and women. Many women decide to have children, which will obviously take them out of the workforce for some time. Many of those women also choose to stay at home with their newborn while the child's father works. By doing this, the woman misses out on the experience and hours needed for a promotion or raise, while her male counterpart stayed at work and probably gained experience needed for a promotion or raise. However, this was their choice. Nobody forced the couple to have a child and decide that the mother should stay home. The father could have stayed home if that's what the couple had decided upon, and that is *solely* the couple's decision to make. It's actually sexist to get upset when women decide to stay home while trying to push them away from this choice. It isn't sexist to let couples decide what's best for their own situation.

Women also tend to make different career path choices. This is why you do not find many women in upper-level computer science or engineering classes on college campuses. The market will just naturally pay an engineer of any gender more than a librarian of any gender. But where is the gender equality in mining jobs? What about other jobs that require a lot of physical strength? Why are women not flocking to these jobs? Maybe because they are not willing to do them, but men are. These are simply choices being made by individual people, and pushing them to make other decisions is an infringement on their liberty.

Feminism was supposed to liberate women to make their own decisions, but it has morphed into something that is trying to force women into roles they may not choose, all the while claiming that if they choose to take a more traditional role, they are not actually women. The free market does not care what role women take in society. If someone wants to be a housewife, then great. If someone else wants to become a scientist, then also great. Either choice should be theirs to make, but modern feminism has too often shamed women for making the former.

When it comes to allegations of a patriarchal society run by men, something seems off, considering that women graduate college at a higher rate than men, more women are enrolled in college than men, and women hold more of the country's master's degrees, law degrees, and doctoral degrees than men.[13] It seems odd that a patriarchal society that hates women would offer them so many opportunities. The truth is that women are seeking these opportunities, and are getting them, because there is no grand conspiracy hindering them. Women actually make more than their male counterparts when both are in their twenties.[14] However, the circumstances switch when women enter into their thirties, a time when many women *choose* to have children.

Still, the best argument against the gender wage gap is the fact that men still have jobs. If women could really be paid 77 percent of what men are paid for the same job and quality of work, then every business owner that hires a man would be incompetent. They should hire all women and use the 23 percent that they save to invest back into their business to beat their competition or simply to become wealthier. Then men would be forced to take that same lower wage, or not have any job at all. This is just how the world works. The truth is that men are not paid more for the same exact work as women; *people* are paid more for longer hours and certain career choices—choices that are theirs to make, not choices to be made by some politician.

People trying to earn a living in a free market have a disincentive to discriminate. If they do, they lose the core of capitalism, which is cash. A twenty-dollar bill is a twenty-dollar bill whether it comes from a white man or a black woman. Capitalism only cares about cash, and nothing else.

Free markets regulate things like racism and sexism by themselves. Because despite what any politician may say, our land is not riddled with racism and sexism. Sure, there are some bad people, but they are few and far between and, like we discussed, generally not tolerated in the United States. But under big government, it only takes one evil person—the leader—for the whole country to become evil. Many Germans believed that Hitler was a great man who would really make them better off. This one man was able to nearly exterminate an entire ethnic group and nearly expand his murderous regime across the world.

Bigots cannot last for long in a free market. This is because discrimination is very expensive in a free market. If we define racism as using skin color or ethnicity as a measure for people, government policies such as affirmative action are racist, because two minority groups are actually hurt by affirmative action, Asians and Jews.[15] If the goal is to eliminate racism, why would we enact race-based policies? Because of what affirmative action is, it requires discriminating against *some* race. That's no way to end racism.

When two governments meet each other for the first time, they size each other up to see if one can steal the other's resources through war. When two capitalists meet for the first time, they trade.

QUICK-DRAW POINTS:

- Capitalism forces racists out of their positions and acts as a barrier against them.

- Capitalism couldn't care less about what color someone's skin is. It only cares about cash.

- Racism put in place by the government is still racism.

- If it were true that one could pay women seventy-seven cents to every dollar they pay a man for the exact same work, anyone who hired a man would be making a horrible business decision and would be run out of business by someone smart enough to take advantage of these savings.

- A woman's choice of career or life path is only her business—and not the business of a politician or political movement. Likewise, if a woman makes the choice to work in an industry that statistically does not pay as well as others, that is her choice alone and no one else's.

3. REGULATIONS, MANDATES, AND THOSE DARNED MONOPOLIES

Supporters of big government claim that we need to regulate businesses in order to help out the little guy. They claim that true, unregulated capitalism allows the rich to exploit the poor. However, in reality, regulations actually hurt the little guy, because they allow those on top to remain there with less effort. Another argument for regulations and mandates is that they keep a company from expanding too much, to the point where it owns everything. Of course, nobody would want this. However, we will see how regulations and mandates actually create an environment that makes such expansion by a single company easier. Supporters of a bigger government also like to mandate that businesses provide benefits such as health care, paid maternity leave, a maximum amount of regular work hours, etc. We will get to all of these points shortly.

But first, let's start with red tape. Regulations

are intended to keep big companies at bay so they do not take over the entire economy, become a monopoly, or basically become the government themselves. However, when a regulation is slapped on an industry, it's the big guys who are happy. When a new rule comes down on beverage companies, Coca-Cola and Pepsi lick their lips. No longer will they have to worry about the little guy in their garage creating a better soda, because this person in their garage cannot cut through all the red tape or afford the government mandates in order to compete with them.

Here's another example. When the Environmental Protection Agency decided it would require contractors and home remodelers to follow new procedures in order to deal with lead paint after it was discovered to be harmful to human health, small businesses took the biggest hit. The new procedures cost thousands of dollars to comply with, and some contracting and remodeling businesses were simply unable to cover the costs. Job losses followed, and bigger companies, who could afford to implement the government-mandated changes, increased their share of the market.[16] Not only that, but many contractors also started to consider just ignoring the procedures, because there was no way to afford them.

Now let's return to the soft drink industry. What if it was discovered that when aluminum cans come in contact with corn syrup they produce a chemical just as harmful as lead? Regulations would probably follow, but what if these regulations cast a huge cost on the companies, like they did in the previous example? Coke and Pepsi could probably take the hit, but younger and smaller companies may not be able to keep up. This is quite all right with Coke and Pepsi, because even though they must shell out more cash to comply with the regulation, they will also get a bigger share of the market.

One might argue that without this new regulation, soft drink companies would never do anything to improve the safety of their products because of the cost. While this may be true at first, would you still buy soda from companies that did not? Probably not. The companies that do correct the situation, however, would retain their business. So, in a sense, companies have incentive to regulate themselves in some situations.

Imagine if the EPA had never regulated the market like they did in response to the findings about lead paint. In this situation, nobody would have forced home repair and remodeling companies to deal with lead paint in a certain way. You may counter that this would be horrible, since lead would still be used in our paint, and many workers would be exposed to it while painting. But would companies really get away with allowing this? Would new homeowners simply allow lead paint to exist in their homes? Maybe some people would be willing to take the risk, but the only people they would be hurting are themselves. The people who wanted the lead out of their homes would pay the cost for it to be removed in a way that would become more efficient and cheap as the market adjusted. But by forcing companies into a new, costly routine so quickly, the EPA put many people's jobs and livelihoods at risk, while the free market would have ensured these changes took place naturally over time.

When the government mandates new workplace regulations for an entire industry, the small businesses that cannot afford the changes, but still treat their employees very well, are often pushed out. Left behind are the big corporations that can afford the changes, and in many cases, were already meeting these conditions with their workers. This is because they can afford it, while the small companies in those industries cannot. Forcing companies to provide certain work conditions is a violation of their autonomy. If one company offers work conditions that are simply impossible to endure, nobody will work for them. Potential employees will go to other companies, and the company that was unwilling to offer adequate conditions will go out of business. In the end, people are smart and will do what is best for them. People are not sheep that need to be led around by the government. If you are offered a job at a firm where all the walls just happen to be electrified, you are not forced to work there. You can just back out and find another firm.

Sometimes regulations can wipe an entire industry out. For example, in 2016 the ride share apps Uber and Lyft terminated all services in Austin, Texas. They did this because the city demanded

REGULATIONS, MANDATES, AND THOSE DARNED MONOPOLIES

that they do fingerprint background checks on all of their drivers rather than the third-party background checks they were already using. The companies claimed that the new measures would simply be too time-consuming and expensive for them to enact. Because of this regulation, ten thousand drivers lost their part-time or full-time job, and the entire city lost a great service that is extremely useful in big cities like Austin.[17] Now imagine if the federal government had mandated this all across the land.

Another infamous modern government regulation is the Obamacare mandate that forced businesses with fifty or more full-time employees to provide health care for all of their full-time employees. This is another instance where the little people got hurt. Many huge companies like Google or Ford were already offering health care to employees in their compensation plans. Who was hit hardest by this mandate? Small businesses. The businesses that could afford to pay for fifty salaries, but not fifty health care plans, were put into a very tough situation. Many had to cut hours for their employees in order to stay under the "fifty-person" threshold.[18] This mandate not only hurt businesses that were hoping to expand, hire more employees, and provide more goods and services, but it also hurt the families of the people employed at those businesses. These people now had to live on less and, in many cases, pick up a second or third job. Some small businesses had to contract or go out of business completely.

And, again, this left the huge companies that could already afford to comply with the regulation standing. Once again, some young entrepreneurs' dreams of becoming the next Henry Ford, Bill Gates, or Jeff Bezos were shattered by big government.

The Obamacare mandate did not only hurt small businesses with over fifty full-time employees, though. Many businesses with a little less than fifty full-time employees felt they could not scale up to fifty employees (or higher). This means that many potential jobs were not created because some small businesses could not afford the mandate.[19] This hurts the business, the potential employee, *and* the consumer. Of course, there were still businesses that expanded past the 50-employee threshold. But for those that did not but could have, this was a case of the government holding them back from something when a free market would not have.

The consumer cannot be forgotten in this situation, either. When Senators Bernie Sanders and Ted Cruz debated health care on CNN in early February 2017, a woman who owned a hair salon complained to Sanders that the Obamacare mandate was just too much for her to handle in a business where profit margins are already thin.[20] If small businesses like these are pushed out, whole communities will lose their local businesses and be forced to rely on larger companies.

Another potential mandate that has been winning hearts is paid maternity leave. This would require businesses to pay women some salary while they are on leave after having a child. Obviously this would be an expense for any business, as they would be paying someone without them producing anything. It is not at all ethical to force an employer to pay for a baby that someone else wanted to have. The employer may choose to do this, but that is their prerogative—it's not their responsibility to provide for someone who is not coming to work. However, if they do choose to offer this, more power to them. Just like many companies use paid vacation as an incentive for potential employees, paid maternity leave can also be a great incentive. But this should be for the business owner(s) to decide.

Let's also look at whether or not the government should pay for the leave. When the "government" pays, it is actually the people who are paying, not the government. So, if we were to have a system where the government gives paid maternity leave, someone on the West Coast who took unpaid leave to raise their kids would now have to pay for someone on the East Coast to raise theirs. Those people on the West Coast should not be forced to pay for something they had no part in. They should be allowed to keep the money they earn and spend it on whatever *they* want, not on what a politician wants.

Big companies know that paid maternity leave is a good bargaining chip when it comes to getting great talent. It turns out that big companies like Adobe, Facebook, Google, Apple, and Microsoft, to name a few, already have the greatest paid maternity leave programs in the country.[21] So, again, it turns out that this policy would keep the big companies in control and hold smaller businesses down. Not only that, but this regulation is asking for actual hiring discrimination based on sex. If a small business is forced to offer paid maternity leave to a woman but cannot afford it, they will intentionally not hire women of childbearing age. This does not make the small business unethical; it just means they are trying to survive. The mandate is unethical. Not only would a regulation like this be an attack on small businesses and potential employees, but also an attack on women because it forces smaller employers to be wary of hiring women.

The biggest loser from regulations is the small business, which is the heart of the American economy. 54 percent of all sales in the United States come from small businesses, and they also provide 55 percent of the jobs in our economy.[22] We cannot afford to kill them with regulations. Under President Reagan, regulations were rolled back quite a bit in the 1980s, creating 19 million new jobs, according to the Heritage Foundation.[23] Today, there is a plethora of regulations that small businesses must cut through in order to operate.[24] Many of these take much-needed time away from the businesses forced to comply with them.

One big regulation that gives businesses a hard time is the distinction between independent contractors and employees (a major issue for companies such

REGULATIONS, MANDATES, AND THOSE DARNED MONOPOLIES

as Uber). This matters because actual employees are protected by policies governing minimum wage, regular work hours, and worker's compensation whereas a contracted "employee" is not. This is an issue for Uber because the line between whether drivers work for Uber, or are just contracted out to pick up Uber's users, is blurry. A huge company like Uber can spend the money to create a new department to handle these employment-related issues, but a small business cannot afford to have someone else handle them. In other words, a huge company could easily just hire a legal team to sift through the law or even defend itself in a court battle, but a smaller business would probably not be able to afford such luxuries. Big-government supporters tend to dislike huge companies because of the massive amounts of wealth that they create, so you would think that they would try to help the small business. Unfortunately, despite their attempt to hamper big companies with regulations, they wind up hurting the small businesses the most.

These are just a couple of examples of how government regulations do the exact opposite of what they promise. Big government is toted around as the ultimate savior that will liberate the people from oppressive companies, when in reality it keeps the average citizen down, allowing big companies to enjoy less competition and more power. The free market, on the other hand, does not force any business (or person) to do anything, which allows for more wealth creation for all. Without regulations, small businesses are better able to grow and challenge bigger companies, and more well-paying jobs are created as the competition for customers and consumers becomes more heated. When the government suffocates smaller businesses, huge corporations are left without any competition. This situation can potentially lead to monopolies of all kinds.

QUICK-DRAW POINTS:

- Government actions aimed at preventing huge companies from gaining too much power ironically create an environment where that exact outcome is more likely to occur.

- When a government tries to regulate something in the name of public safety it is often unnecessary. The free market would have naturally regulated it, because people do not want to purchase or own things that can harm them. Like in the case of lead paint, people would begin to stop buying paint with lead in it. The paint companies that make paint with lead in it would go out of business, and contracting companies would learn how to safely remove the paint because there is a demand for their services.

- Regulations and mandates kill jobs, especially when it comes to small businesses, which provide the majority of American jobs.

- Many big corporations already offer great benefits to their employees like paid maternity leave, more vacation time, and health care. Small businesses have trouble offering

REGULATIONS, MANDATES, AND THOSE DARNED MONOPOLIES

these things because they simply do not make as much money. Forcing small businesses to do these things will put many people out of work.

- Regulations and mandates keep potential businesses out of the market. The person crafting the next best cola in their garage cannot afford to traverse the minefield that is the regulatory landscape, and thus we will never see that product being offered in the market.

4. CAPITALISM SATISFIES DEMAND— COMMUNISM BRINGS STARVATION

There is a Soviet joke made famous by President Reagan that goes like this:

A man goes to the agency that handles the distribution of cars in the country. He gives the clerk the money for the car, and the man is told he can pick the car up in ten years.

"Morning or afternoon?" the man asks the clerk.

"Morning or afternoon?" the clerk repeats. "Ten years from now, what difference does it make?"

"Well," the man says, "the plumber is coming in the morning."

Unfortunately for the citizens of the Soviet Union, this was not far from the truth. If you tried to tell the joke in reference to the American economy, however, you would receive blank stares. Why? Because a plumber can usually come within a day or two, and we can drive a car off the lot after purchasing it. There is a reason we can enjoy these luxuries,

CAPITALISM SATISFIES DEMAND – COMMUNISM BRINGS STARVATION

and, you guessed it, the reason is capitalism.

Capitalism satisfies people's demands while communism creates shortages. Soviet citizens would stand in line for several hours every day, if not overnight, just to get bread for their families.[25] In the United States, the longest we have to wait for bread is a couple of minutes for the lines to die down at the cash registers. That is, if there are any lines during our visit. Yet some still claim that capitalism has failed the people and a bigger, more broad government is the answer.

Some question why we need twenty-three different types of deodorants.[26] Maybe it's because there is demand for different types of deodorant. Not only that, but deodorant companies compete with each other to make increasingly better products at the lowest price possible. Under communism, you would use the deodorant of the leader's choice, not what you would prefer. Some guys like Old Spice, while others prefer Degree. There's nothing wrong with that, and it's probably a good thing that we all have different preferences.

This is the same reason why we have several different car companies and styles to choose from when purchasing a car. The Soviet Union had one major car manufacturer for ordinary citizens. This was the Lada, and it was not exactly a Mercedes, as it was designed to be produced extremely cheaply and quickly.[27] In the United States, not only can we choose among several domestic car manufacturers, we can even buy cars that come from other countries if we want. Most car companies around the world make cars that are affordable to a middle-class American. An American does not only have one choice; some might prefer a Silverado over an Accord. This gives consumers more choices and the freedom to spend their money how they see fit, rather than how a politician tells them they should spend it.

Another advantage of the market system over pure socialism or communism is the fact that if a product is not good enough, or if people simply do not like what is being offered, nobody has to pay for it, and eventually the product will leave the market. Imagine a deodorant in a free market that smells like an actual landfill. Obviously, not many people would buy this product and it would be removed from the shelves after some time. However, in a completely government-run economy, if you are even lucky enough to find that deodorant on the shelves, landfill scent could be your only option. The point is that in a government run economy, your choice of products is, by law, the leader's choice of products.

Bernie Sanders once claimed that bread lines were a good thing, because, in his view, in "other countries" with no bread lines, the rich were eating while the poor were starving to death.[28] Clearly, in the United States, we have no bread lines, and our poor are not starving to death in mass numbers. But it just so happens that in countries where bread lines are the norm, the leaders are typically not the ones waiting in line.

CAPITALISM SATISFIES DEMAND – COMMUNISM BRINGS STARVATION

In government-run economies, people who produce goods have quotas or are paid based on the amount they produce rather than the quality of their offerings. This means that farmers no longer avoid sending bad fruit to market, as a worm-ridden pear will fetch the same amount of money as a perfect one. Since government-run economies lead to shortages, people are basically forced to eat the worm-ridden pears or not eat at all. In a free market, the farmer that sends bad pears doesn't make money, because there is demand for good pears and farmers will fill that demand or not be paid at all.

Do not fall for the line that those *other* leaders were flawed, but *this one* is better and will do a good job. It is a lie. In Cuba, Venezuela, North Korea, and every country where pure socialism or communism has been attempted, the people were or are starving. Some on the Left may like the idea of bread lines, but the truth is that bread lines are a horrible situation to be in. We should be thankful that in America we can go to the store to pick up ingredients for dinner and be back home in under thirty minutes.

QUICK-DRAW POINTS:

- Free markets offer choices. Choices between which deodorant you want to wear, what soft drinks you want to consume, and which brand of car you want to drive. Government-run markets often only offer one choice: the government's brand of everything.

A MORAL CASE FOR CAPITALISM

- Government-run economies provide their people with shortages of essential items. Free markets provide their people with overstocked shelves and a plethora of items that nobody would consider "essential."

- It is no coincidence that in the government-run economies of countries such as Venezuela and North Korea, the people starve while the government officials are well fed. That's how those economies are structured. (The same was true of the Soviet Union.)

- Free markets create competition. This naturally leads to better quality products at a lower price, and no law had to be implemented to create this outcome.

- In free markets, people can waste. Nobody encourages waste, but in free markets, there is more to go around. In government-run economies, the people cannot waste or else they will die. It is better to live in a society that can tolerate waste than one that would suffer greatly if it did.

5. TAXES AND GOVERNMENT SPENDING

Some people often wonder what our Founding Fathers would think of America today. No doubt they would be pleased to see that we are still a nation, but would they be entirely happy with our condition? Certainly not when it comes to taxes. Our current tax rates, and the amount of different taxes, would be a disgrace to those Sons of Liberty who fought tyranny some 250 years ago. As a reminder, the Boston Tea Party was staged to protest a 3 percent tax.[29] This is both hilarious and sad when you look at the fact that the average American's income tax rate is 30 percent.[30] Not to mention taxes on air travel, hotels, gas, property, gifts, Social Security, marriage, imports, emissions, businesses, and other taxes that could fill up a couple of pages. The Sons of Liberty resisted a 3 percent tax, and now we have politicians running the country who are not opposed to a 90 percent tax rate.[31] So, no, our Founding Fathers would not be entirely happy with our condition.

Federal taxes aren't the only problem. There are also state and local taxes, which, in many cases, effectively tax people three times. People get up every morning for work in order to pay the bills, but are then taxed at every step throughout their day. And yet our government is still in debt.

Additionally, every time Congress runs a deficit, they are foisting the bill onto the next generation of Americans. Are we not obligated to create a better country for those coming behind us? Or do we just not care anymore? Should we just let the next generation worry about it since we'll be dead, anyway? If generations continue to allow government debt to increase, they will continue to push that bill onto their kids. Eventually someone is going to have to pay that bill, since we cannot spend someone else's money forever. Eventually creditors will ask for their money back; who will pay then? This is the question we should be asking politicians who support both tax cuts *and* increased spending. Sure, the economy would likely boom from the tax cuts and the increased spending would help provide more government projects like infrastructure and useless bureaucracies, but what about the next generation? How will they pay all that money off and still maintain their own living standards?

A big problem with government spending is that once it starts, it is very hard to stop and extremely easy to expand. It's difficult to convince someone to relinquish a subsidy that helps them, but very easy to convince them to receive more "free" stuff paid for by someone else. This is how government grows to control its people. It would be considered political suicide to completely scrap programs like welfare. But if someone promises universal health care, their following grows.

When it comes to taxes and government spending, some people might be forced to pay for something that does not apply to them or that they do not agree with. Health care is one example. Someone who has always been very healthy and has taken care of their body will be forced to pay for the health services of someone that did not. If the healthy person wants to donate money to a health charity, then that's great, and we hope they do. But when they are being *forced* to give that money up, that is theft. People should be allowed to spend their money on what they think is best for them, not what a politician claims is best for them.

Another example would be someone who is pro-life being forced to give funds to institutions that provide abortions such as Planned Parenthood. Would a pro-gun-control voter like it if they were forced to pay for someone's gun through their taxes? No. It's not fair in either case. Obviously, the first person would never willingly choose to fund an abortion and the second would never spend money on a gun, but now they are being forced to. This is the theme of the entire book: either people are allowed to do as they wish within the scope of the law, or they are coerced into paying for policies and luxuries that may not even help them, or that they may not agree with, simply because the government has the threat of force in its back pocket.

But let's be fair here. Voters on the Right tend to favor a free market as well as a strong defense. In my opinion, national security is the number one priority of the government, but there are people on the other side of the aisle who would like to see a reduction in the size of our military. Just like taxing the pro-life voter in order to fund Planned Parenthood is something we need to consider, we should also consider how we tax the military skeptic to fund a military. We can go on and on about whether or not the military, Planned Parenthood, or both are necessities; the larger point, however, is about coercion, and how taxes facilitate it.

But what about the rich, big corporations and hedge-fund babies in our country? Should they pay a higher percentage of their income than someone who creates less wealth?

It seems fair to many people to have richer folks pay a higher percentage of their wages in taxes. This is why a progressive tax is popular among many people. A progressive tax is where the higher your income, the higher percentage you pay in taxes. People feel this is an acceptable way to operate since the rich have more to give. However, progressive taxes are no more justifiable than regressive taxes. Regressive taxation is when the less money one makes, the higher their tax burden becomes. This would mean someone making $40,000 every year would pay a higher percentage of taxes on their income than someone making $50,000 would. The absolute amount the person making $40,000 a year pays may be less than the amount the person making $50,000 pays, but as a percentage of their income, the person who makes less has a higher relative tax burden. The point is, these two systems are not fair, as both of them favor one income over the other. The progressive tax favors those who make less and punishes those who make more. The regressive tax favors those who make more and punishes those who make less.

This is why, in my opinion, a flat tax is the only fair way to tax people. With a flat tax, everyone would pay the same percentage of their income in taxes. If we think of income as a pie that someone bakes each year, the government taxes the pie by taking a slice for its greedy self. With a flat tax, everyone gives up the same percentage of their pie each year instead of giving up a greater percentage simply because they baked a bigger pie. Why would we ever want to discourage or punish success? If anything, it should be encouraged.

Another argument for a flat tax is the fact that with our current system, huge companies can hire a stellar team of accountants and lawyers in order to navigate tax loopholes. This is something that small businesses cannot afford to do. With a simple flat tax, there are no loopholes: One simply pays the percentage that is required of them. This eliminates the ability of big businesses to avoid taxes that small businesses, and the average citizen, cannot.

You hear many politicians talking about the tax loopholes. This talk comes from both sides of the aisle, but rarely does anyone offer a solution that would work. Ted Cruz was hammered for his proposal of a 10 percent flat tax on all personal income. However, this is a plan that would have evaporated tax loopholes. It's simple: You pay 10 percent of what you made. There are no loopholes. But, of course, many politicians tote around the idea of higher taxes and more red tape to close the loopholes. This will only create more loopholes and make it harder for the little guy to succeed because they cannot afford to navigate these loopholes.

Our tax code is over two million words long. This makes it next to impossible for the average person or small business to successfully navigate it on their own. Collectively, Americans also spent nearly nine billion hours on taxes alone in 2016.[32] With a simple flat tax, it would only take a few minutes to calculate the percentage in question. Then our economy could get back to creating wealth rather than engaging in the time and energy suck that is taxes.

Taxes create poverty, slow technological development, suffocate innovation, and destroy people's will. When a new tax touches a small business, there will have to be adjustments in order to account for it. These adjustments could come in the form of laying off employees, a rise in prices of the products the business produces, a decrease in the quality of the business's product, pay decreases for some employees, or the outright shutdown of the business. Not only will one or more of these things likely happen, but the business will most likely have to stop expanding and hiring more employees. This means an end to job creation and opportunity—all in the name of opportunity and job creation. Funny how that works when the government gets involved.

Taxes make it difficult for a small business to expand, which in turn makes it difficult to hire new workers. These workers, who are looking for jobs that don't exist, then must rely on the government to put food on the table. Remember from earlier that the vast majority of government actions end up creating more people who rely on the government. When taxes are raised, the economy is slowed and more people become reliant on government safety nets. When those safety nets need to be expanded to cover more people, they require more funding from more taxes, and the cycle continues.

There would otherwise be no need for these government policies. If people do not suffer and are not forced into poverty because taxes ran all the businesses where they live out of town, there would be no need for political parties supportive of government expansion in any country. Thus, politicians in parties that support government expansion have an interest in expanding the lower class in order to increase their voting base. Whether they do it with this purpose in mind or not is between them and their conscience, but it happens either way and there is no excuse for it.

Supporters of wealth redistribution may believe that taking from Person A in order to give to Person B, who is poor, is a noble cause. This is because the vast majority of supporters believe that redistribution is solely done in order to help poor people. But why should anyone be forced to give up something they earned just because someone else did not? Steve Jobs did not become rich because he was some lucky guy who had a vast conspiracy pulling for him. He became rich because he sold something that everyone in the world wanted. Besides, it has never been acceptable for a person to benefit from the labor of someone else at no cost. We once fought a civil war in this country over this very idea. The principle does not change whether it is the government or a private citizen applying the force.

Another question to ask is, does wealth redistribution actually help poor people in the way intended? Throughout this book we have discussed whether or not a poor person in this kind of situation is helped by government interventions. In most cases, the answer is a resounding "no." When provided for by the government, that poor person has less incentive to produce. And when taxed more, a rich person also has less incentive to produce.

Of course, some taxes are warranted. Without a police force many of our streets would be in chaos, and without a military we would likely be part of the Soviet Union, and these words that I write would be illegal. So, it's not that all taxes are bad, but we are missing the mark by a very, very large margin.

Taxes are essentially armed robbery: The government has tanks; you do not. You are not going to win that fight if you attempt to not pay your taxes. Obviously, the government is not going to invade your home if you do not pay your taxes, but resist long enough, and force will be used. Even though you work all day for your wages and use your own talents and abilities to earn them, the government thinks it is entitled to those wages. And besides, politicians need to pay for the promises they made on the campaign trail. Truthfully, the government is not entitled to your wages, and any politician that supports tax hikes simply believes that they own you and your labor and can decide what is done with them. Remember, you pay the salaries of government officials. You don't work for them; they work for you.

QUICK-DRAW POINTS:

- Taxes will destroy a country. They kill business, jobs, incentives, and the desire to succeed.

- When you tax a voter to fund a project that they might not even agree with, you are forcing them into an agreement they would have otherwise not entered.

A MORAL CASE FOR CAPITALISM

- If you want to eliminate tax loopholes for good, create a flat tax. You pay the agreed-upon percentage of your income; nothing more, nothing less. If you want to keep creating loopholes, follow politicians that want to reform the tax code in another way.

- Taxes are all about force. If you do not pay your taxes, force will be used in order to get the money eventually. This is not liberty—this is tyranny.

6. TECHNOLOGICAL ADVANCEMENTS BRING BIG REWARDS FOR ALL

The thought of computers or machines taking people's jobs has become a common talking point. Sure, a program that can do your taxes in a few seconds will put many accountants out of a job, and this will result in short-term job losses. However, this change is beneficial to everyone in the long term, and the lost number of jobs will eventually be regained. Technological advancements may make jobs in a certain industry irrelevant in the short term, but they also create new jobs in different sectors while at the same time making the lives of everyone better.

The world witnessed this principle in action when the American automobile industry became established, rendering the horse and buggy industry more or less useless. Henry Ford first finished production of the Model T in the early 1900s. There were cars that preceded the Model T, but they were a rich man's toy, as very few could afford one. Ford was able to improve the existing offerings through innovation, so much so that Americans from all walks of life were able to own a car. This was due to his famous business strategy: the assembly line.

As car ownership flourished, many horse and buggy-related companies began to shut down. This, of course, sent many people home without a job. So, in the short term some people did lose their jobs to the automobile, but that is only one part of the picture. Some horse and buggy-related companies were able to stay in business by adjusting themselves to the new reality of automobiles, and these workers were able to keep their jobs. Also, the new demand for automobiles created new job openings that the old horse and buggy workers shifted to fill. But the biggest part of the picture is arguably the fact that people now had cars. This made life much more simple for people, as cars did not die as quickly as horses, required less maintenance, were faster, and did not need to rest. Everyone's life was made better from this technological advancement. Thanks to Ford's early pioneering, there were roughly 1.8 cars per household in the United States in 2013.[33]

But what about the industries that may not be able to recover from a major disruption? For example, the demand for horses dropped significantly because of the automobile, and many horse breeders lost their jobs. For a short time, these people were out of work, but, again, new jobs were created that centered around the automobile. A quick look at

TECHNOLOGICAL ADVANCEMENTS BRING BIG REWARDS FOR ALL

statistics illustrates how technology and job types are constantly evolving—and why this is a good thing. According to the Bureau of Labor Statistics, in March 2017 the unemployment rate was 4.5 percent.[34] We know that this number will fluctuate naturally no matter what we do, but if technological advancements really destroyed jobs, would our unemployment rate really be 4.5 percent at this point in human history? Think back to when the only tools humans had were two hands, a rock, and some sticks. Obviously, we have come a very long way since then, but if technology destroyed jobs, should we not see an unemployment rate closer to 100 percent? Since 1947, the unemployment rate in the United States has fluctuated, but it has never gone above 10 percent.[35] We have had tremendous technological advancements since 1947 (iPhones, electric cars, flat-screen TVs, self-driving tractors, and so on), but our unemployment rate is still under 10 percent. It's obvious that technology does not permanently kill jobs.

We should also look at what new technologies and inventions do for everyone. As mentioned earlier, cars were once exclusive to the rich. Today, 88 percent of households in the United States own at least one car.[36] No longer is it a luxury only for the rich.

Another example is cell phones. The first working cell phone was created in 1973. It looked like a brick and was as heavy as one, too. In 1983 they went on sale in the United States at a price of about $4,000 (around $9,700 today, adjusting for inflation).[37] Like the automobile, the cell phone was another rich man's toy when it came out. Things have changed since then. According to the Pew Research Center, 92 percent of adults in the United States owned a cell phone in 2015.[38] It is no longer a rich person's luxury. In fact, today, many cellular carriers even offer free phones if you sign a contract with them (a slight price drop from $9,700). Additionally, you can purchase an iPhone 7 for less than $600. Still a pretty penny, but much, much less than the cost of the first phones—and with a whole lot more functionality.

Indeed, it's important to note how much cell phone technology has advanced as well. The first cell phones could painstakingly make a call and hold a charge, but now phones can text, email, surf the internet, take a picture of your food, light your room at night, entertain you with games and videos, play your favorite songs, etc. All of this thanks to "evil" capitalists. Yes, Apple turns a huge profit on creating and selling its phones, but we also get an amazing product that makes life so much simpler. The relationship is mutually beneficial: Apple is monetarily rewarded for their risk and success, and we get a great product which, at one point, would have been the size of a living room, but can now fit in our pockets.

These benefits are not exclusive to things like iPhones. Medicine also benefits from technological advancements. There are, for example, companies that make machines that can follow a doctor's commands in order to perform surgery. Since

TECHNOLOGICAL ADVANCEMENTS BRING BIG REWARDS FOR ALL

these machines don't have to worry about shaky hands or a possible sneeze, they can be more reliable than human hands. They are the first step towards machines that can perform surgery on their own with no guidance. In the future, these will lower surgical costs, as robots do not need to go to medical school, and we can build as many of them as we need. We just hope that whoever programs their actions does go to medical school.

A new tractor that can harvest wheat three times faster than an outdated one, or a new fertilizer that can help yield twice as much wheat in a given season, will lower the cost of bread and other wheat products for everyone. All this is thanks to someone who made an advancement in technology or science. Why did they make this advancement? Well, they were incentivized to do so by a free market that they knew would compensate them well for their new product. The new fertilizer company might put other companies out of business, or hurt their sales, but should we really stop the new company because of that? Thanks to them, we can feed more people at a lower cost—and it's not the fault of the new company if older companies can't keep up.

Ford's assembly line business model allowed for cars to be created so cheaply and quickly that the average person could afford one. Not only could the average person afford one, but they could also use the money they saved from purchasing the cheaper product on something else. Whether this went toward their personal savings, a different consumer product (whose purchase would lead to the creation of more jobs), or starting a company of their own, the entire economy became wealthier because of Ford's innovations. You can see now how a new technology or business model makes an entire economy better off – not just those who made the advancement.

Big government thwarts technological advancement in different ways. One way, as discussed above, is through regulations. In a heavily regulated industry, companies must tread lightly, as though they were walking through a minefield, in order to operate. This can force smaller companies to spend extra time weaving through legal barbed wire. Larger companies can just pay a legal team, but this is still another expense they must allocate from their budget.

Onerous regulations can be especially harmful to smaller firms and companies. Since they are small, they cannot delegate these problems to a legal team and must spend time and energy to avoid them. This means less time and energy will go toward the advancement of their specific technology, product, or service. This is how huge corporations keep smaller ones down. The family owned restaurant in your town does not have lobbyists in D.C., but McDonald's has plenty of them.

Another way big government kills technological advancements is through the destruction of incentives. In a capitalist society, people know that great new ideas and products are rewarded with cash. In a government-run economy, there is no such reward. A new product or idea, if it were to even appear, would instantly be owned by the state and not the individual. So, there would be no point for anyone to spend a lot of time or effort on creating a better product.

Imagine an inventor in a state-run economy. They work a normal 9–5 shift and have a great idea for the next life-changing product. What incentive do they have to come home from a long day of work and tinker with their design? None, really. Besides pure altruism, they would have no reason to do this. And the fact that there is no food on the shelves at the supermarket, a frequent occurrence in government-run economies, would really reinforce the futility of their labor and sink their moral. Even if they were able to figure this product out and make it great, they would not even own it and would not be compensated for their risk, so what's the point?

Since there is no incentive to invent new products and technologies in a government-run economy, these economies do not advance. They take what technology they have and keep it. This is why the Lada never really changed in the Soviet Union over many decades and why you won't see the next life-changing product emerge from Venezuela.

We saw how much mass production of the automobile aided humanity. We cannot even begin to conceive what advancements lay ahead, but they will only emerge if there is an incentive for their conception. Just think how much human health has been helped by technology. Modern plumbing, waste disposal, and medicine have made us exponentially healthier than humans living just a hundred years ago. We obviously shouldn't stop making these advancements simply because some jobs may be lost in the short term. Should we trade in our modern automobiles with air conditioning for horses and buggies just so people in that (now forgotten) industry can have jobs?

Is it possible to envision a world where literally every working task is performed by a machine? A world where there are simply no jobs because a computer or robot has fulfilled every assignment? Of course there is, but all of our needs would be fulfilled. Nobody would even need a job in this world because everything would be produced for free by the vast network of machines.

Ironically, this vast utopia where everyone is taken care of and everyone is equal—the very utopia that communists call for—can only be achieved through capitalism. We have modern cars, phones, medicine, and other gadgets because of economic incentives. It is delusional to believe that people risking it all to start a new company are just doing it for the fun of it. Monetary incentives play a major role.

As with most things, governments need to stay out of the way of most, if not all, industries. New companies and owners should be allowed to rise without being stifled by regulations. Technology advances more quickly this way because companies need to constantly one-up each other with better products in order to win over consumers. Without competition, Louis Chevrolet would have never come along to make a better product than Ford.

QUICK-DRAW POINTS:

- If it were true that technological advancements destroyed jobs in the long run, none of us would have a job, considering how far we've come since using sticks and stones.

- Tech advancements make for a better world. Each year our cars get better and safer, our air conditioning units become more efficient, and our medicine becomes more life changing. This is not something we should stop or slow.

- Because of capitalism, even the poor in America have access to things like cell-phones, TVs, and climate control—things that poor people (and rich people) of a hundred years ago could have never dreamed of having.

- Technology can, and will, one day feed the entire world. But only if it is left to grow without the government getting its sticky hands all over it.

- Communism hinders technological advancement, because in a communist economic system there is no longer any incentive to invent anything.

- Tech advancements are the reason why processing equipment that would once fill an entire living room can now fit in your pocket.

A MORAL CASE FOR CAPITALISM

- Tech advancements make things cheaper. For example, currently a select few companies are trying to take people on short trips to space. When this becomes possible, only the very rich will be able to afford it. Give it several years, however, and the middle class will soon be able to join in the fun.

7. HEALTH CARE: THE DREADED TOPIC

Over the past few years, many politicians have increasingly come to support single-payer health care. Let us start by looking at how a single-payer health-care system is funded. Typically, this is done through heavily taxing people in order to pay for services for everyone. This wins votes because it plays to people's emotions. I mean, should the rich not pay for the health care of the person receiving minimum wage?

Taxing the wealthiest among us in order to pay for the health care of all of us is a very seductive policy in the eyes of many people. Because the rich are already rich, right? They should have no problem paying for someone else's health care, because those other people may not be able to afford it and the rich can. Well, should they? And can they actually afford it even though they're rich?

Taking from Person A to pay for the health services of Person B is akin to stealing the labor from

Person A. Person A now has to work extra hours in order to maintain their living standard. Those extra hours go directly to the subsidization of someone else's health bill. In essence, Person A is working, unpaid, for Person B, as Person A is not receiving any benefit from this policy (assuming they are healthy). The only real scenario that would justify this kind of exchange is if there were an outbreak of a horrible infectious disease and curing one person would, in fact, be beneficial to all. But, this is not what we are talking about when it comes to a blanket health-care policy. Some people are pushing for every health issue to be fully covered, for all, by the "government." This means that if someone makes poor eating choices and has fast food for every meal and never exercises, someone else will pay for the consequences of those actions. When the inevitable happens and that person suffers from some sort of health issue due to their poor habits, the bill, and thus the responsibility, is placed on someone else. This isn't right.

Let us assume that Person A and Person B both make similar wages and naturally have a similar tax rate. Now imagine that Person A eats very clean foods and exercises several days a week. However, Person B does not watch what they eat and does not exercise. If Person B were to get sick as a result of this, Person B of course benefits from the free health care, but Person A has been wronged. Person A is forced to pay for the decisions of Person B. Not only that, but Person B does not feel the monetary consequences of their choices. What incentive do they have to change their lifestyle if someone else is going to foot the bill? They have none, other than to avoid becoming sick again.

Now let us look at the situation in another way. We all know people who are naturally quite healthy and some people that are always sick. When the healthy person is forced to pay for health care through taxes, they are not allowed any choice in where their money goes. What if a healthy person does not want to spend money on any sort of health care/insurance for themselves? That money could go to something that they feel is more important to them. Maybe it could help start a new business that creates more jobs or help prop up a philanthropy. Government officials believe they are entitled to your paycheck because you elected them. This is not true. Their job is to protect your liberties. Instead, they treat the people like they don't know what's best for them and the only way to properly spend money is how the government thinks it should be spent. The truth is that you know what is best for you. You know how to handle your life—and money, for that matter—much better than any elitist in Washington, D.C. ever will.

We know that forcing someone to till a field for no pay is unjust, immoral, and utterly disgusting, and forcing someone to work in service of someone else's bills is not very different, in my opinion. Now, of course, actual slaves were and are treated much worse than someone who is taxed, but the logic is the same. The basic concept is that someone is being forced to work outright for someone else without proper compensation.

With a single-payer health-care system, the central government must dictate what is covered and what is not. This is because when something as prized as health care is "free," demand goes through the roof. So, in order to avoid everyone going into the emergency room due to a paper cut, the government needs to set some parameters on what is covered. This means that some health needs will not be sufficiently covered. Maybe there is a shortage of x-rays for broken arms. Because of this, people with broken arms will begin turning to the black market to get help. As well, some things will be covered far too much. That means there will be many doctors just standing around waiting for someone to come in with a certain issue while some other, pressing issue is not addressed. Both of these will happen at once in a single-payer system.

Even the most optimistic numbers from Bernie Sanders's blanket health-care proposal show that federal expenditures would increase by 55 percent.[39] But these numbers do not account for the new demand in the market. No, universal health care would not decrease the use of health care and thus lower the cost. If Lamborghinis suddenly became free overnight, do you think people would buy less or more of them? Or, to put it another way: If health care is perceived as being "free," people would go to the doctor as much as possible, even unnecessarily, because their perception is that they do not need to bear the cost of doing so (Even though in reality, they are paying more in taxes). This means that the minor flu you are suffering from will no longer be a "stay in bed and sleep it off situation" but a "I can go to the doctor because I won't need to pay when I get there" situation.

The free market ensures that supply and demand are in tune. If there are too many dentists in a city, causing a surplus of available dentistry, some will leave because of the lack of business and the high competition. Nobody is forced to pay these extra dentists to stand around in a free market. Likewise, if there are not enough dentists in a city, people will be willing to pay more for dentistry. This will attract new dentists to the city, which will, in turn, decrease the price. You can see now how the free market keeps prices in their fair range. None of the dentists could demand a price that is too high or else another dentist will offer a fair price and take all of the business. The people command the price, really. But in a government run economy, the government commands the price.

The free market also does not require people to pay for someone else's injuries from dangerous hobbies, either. A free-market health-care system requires people to be responsible for themselves and whomever they choose to also be responsible for. For example, we all know people that play it safe and would rather not take any bodily risks such as skydiving or skiing. We all also know people that enjoy taking these risks. The problem is that, many times, these risks can cause bodily harm that can be quite expensive. In a single-payer system, someone that works in an office all day in West Virginia will have to pay the medical bills of an adrenaline junkie in California who keeps breaking bones on the ski slopes. How is this fair? The person playing it safe is now forced to pay for the decisions of someone who chose not to. We wouldn't want the government to ban dangerous recreational activities in order to save money on health care, and we shouldn't want the government to force someone else to pay for those risks.

As mentioned above, single-payer systems give rise to black markets. Black markets are basically illegal markets where people trade for things that the government has banned, restricted, or regulated out of the legitimate market. It arises in response to shortages.

The simplest example is drugs. When the government bans drugs, people will still buy and sell them under the table, because there is enough demand for them. Black markets can be dangerous and expensive because there is no rule of law surrounding them, as they are outside the bounds of the state. This is why health care in Venezuela is so awful. With the government controlling everything, people looking for treatment must turn to the black market, which, in many cases, is more dangerous than the diseases they are seeking treatment for.[40] Lifting the government's sticky hands from the medical market will allow honest doctors to provide the care that people are asking for in a safe environment.

In North Korea, where every single piece of the economy is owned by the state, the black market is the only place where citizens can get decent medical care. This is not surprising. In fact, since the single-payer system in North Korea has failed its people so badly, even official members of the government turn to the black market for medicine. On top of that, overall health in North Korea has actually gotten better with the growth of the black market, because at least the black market offers some sort of incentive to good doctors and treatments.[41] But, in the name of equality, countries like this create an environment where everyone is equal. Because when we all own nothing, we are all truly equal.

Another issue with single-payer systems and those like them is lack of competition.[42] Since everyone is covered and payments are set by the government, doctors, nurses, and hospitals have no reason to become better in order to beat out the competition. In turn, the quality of care becomes worse. This means people will be receiving subpar health care that saps their taxes when they could have received cheap, high-quality health care in a free market. That's not to say, however, that the United States is anywhere near this. Our health care is of pretty good quality all else being equal, but it is certainly not cheap. I believe that the way to increase the quality and decrease the price is through the free market.

If you want our hospitals to operate as efficiently as the DMV, then by all means please bang the drum of socialized health care. If you were to somehow open a free market–style DMV next door to your local government-run DMV, the unending lines at the government-run DMV would disappear overnight, because everyone would be going to the efficient, cheap, free-market DMV next door.

We all know about the sting operations targeting the TSA. In one recent operation, they failed to detect sixty-seven out of seventy illegal items that went through security.[43] The TSA is run by the government. What would happen if these were private companies? They would be out of business—and replaced by competent security companies. However, the government doesn't worry because it believes you cannot fire it or cut it off from its paycheck. Again, it has tanks and you do not. Because of this, government agencies and officials become lax, as they do not fear losing their perch. If you want health care as high quality as the DMV or the TSA, then keep pulling for single-payer.

Single-payer systems can also force people to pay for something they do not support through their taxes. For example, we all remember the Hobby Lobby case where the company opposed paying for contraception on religious grounds.[44] A single-payer system, assuming it covers contraception, would

HEALTH CARE: THE DREADED TOPIC

force a Catholic nun to pay for someone else's contraception, which is against her religion. If we truly have freedom of religion in this country, how could we let this happen?

Many on the Left like to claim that health care is a right. Apparently our Founders must have used invisible ink on the Constitution where it says that health care needs to be "free." First off, health care is not a right. It is something that you can work for if you so desire. Many companies offer health care as a benefit, and someone can also buy it for themselves. This goes back to the discussion on government spending. You wouldn't force Jerry Brown to buy you a Glock, so why are you forced to pay for his doctor's visit? And when someone claims that health care is a right and guns are not, point to the Second Amendment and then ask them to point to the amendment that makes health care a right.

It's no secret that Obamacare caused a rise in premiums.[45] This was such a big issue that one of the Republican candidates in the 2016 presidential race made repealing Obamacare his number one goal. However, what was many people's response to this failing of big government? More government. Most notably, Bernie Sanders touted the idea of single-payer health care. Normally, when you get burned by the stove, you do not turn the heat up. Normally, you would move your hand away and turn the heat down. Not in American politics, apparently; getting burned means we need more heat. It is up to those of us who actually care about the people rather than the power to stop these tyrants before they burn us all.

The free market will admittedly not cover every single person. However, it is the *only* way to keep costs low and give the most people the best care they can receive. There will, of course, be some people that cannot afford a bill. Maybe a child is diagnosed with a horrible disease and the parents simply do not make enough money to cover the costs. This is when we as a community need to step in. Churches, neighborhoods, businesses, etc. need to step in and help these people. I have no doubt that many congregations from multiple religions would love to help someone in need. Many wealthy individuals would also love to help, as most wealthy people in America were not born rich and know what it means to struggle. In these situations, there is no force. That's the difference between government-run health care and health care run by the free market as concerns people who "fall through the gaps." One uses force, the other uses altruism.

QUICK-DRAW POINTS:

- While a government's goal may be to cover every person for every medical procedure, this leads to shortages in the industry and causes very long waiting times just to see a doctor. And when you finally get to see the doctor, the quality of their care is probably going to be quite low, as

HEALTH CARE: THE DREADED TOPIC

they have no incentive to be great. On the other hand, the free market's goal is to provide the best quality health care for the lowest possible price.

- Forcing doctors to perform procedures below the market price is a violation of their autonomy. If a doctor wants to charge idiotically high prices, consumers will go to another doctor. This keeps prices down. If the government ran our health care, we would pay that price and have no other option.

- The DMV sucks—It's okay, you can admit it. We see how the government functions when you just want to get your driver's license. Do we really want it to handle our health?

- Government-run health care *will* increase the price of health care. When something becomes free, more people want it. This increase in demand must be paid for somehow.

8. FREE TRADE MAKES BOTH SIDES BETTER OFF

Recently in American politics, there has been a shift toward a more nationalistic way of thinking when it comes to trade. This is because recent trade deals signed by the American government have given the American people the impression that they are getting the short end of the stick. They feel that all of our jobs and all of our wealth are leaving to go overseas and we have been left with empty factories and wallets. Because of this, politicians from both sides of the aisle have come out in support of tariffs and other protectionist policies in order to keep jobs and money in the United States. However, there is a reason that economists call tariffs "secret taxes." That's because a tariff is exactly that, a tax. And these tariffs/taxes hurt the people of the country that implements them as much as they hurt the other country that is being taxed. To explore this, we will start with simple explanations that will help guide us in

FREE TRADE MAKES BOTH SIDES BETTER OFF

explaining tariffs on an international level.

The first way to explain trade is to point out the fact that each one of us engages in free trade every day. When you awaken in the morning and turn on the light in your room, you are trading. When you turn the shower on, you are trading. When you make breakfast with eggs, toast, and orange juice, you are trading. You are trading when you turn your car on to get to work. You are also trading while performing your job at work.

All of these things you do in the morning to get ready for work require you to pay a fee. The electricity in the room costs money, as does the water, eggs, toast, orange juice, gas, and car payment. You trade your money for these tangible things, and, while you're at work, you trade your labor for money—which you use to trade for all of the things that were just mentioned.

Think about your clothes. It can be safely assumed that you do not make your own clothes. Instead, you go to the store, where you trade your money for clothing. Both sides get what they want in this exchange. The store receives your money, which they use to pay their workers, and you receive the clothes that you need, since, I hate to say it, but nobody wants to see you naked.

In this example, think of yourself and your family as one country, and the store as another country. If you chose to make your own clothes as a family without trade, you would have to find wild sheep somewhere and capture them for their wool. You would also need machines to make metal or plastic buttons for the clothes. You would need sewing material to bind the clothing together. If you were to somehow get your hands on all of these things without trading, you would then have to put in the effort of making the clothes. This would obviously take a very long time.

After several weeks of labor, you could then clothe your family. The only problem is, since you were making the clothes the whole time, there was no food to eat. Assuming that everyone in the family survived this ordeal of not eating for a few weeks, you would all probably decide that maybe trading money for clothes is a better choice. The reason you purchase clothes and other items at the store instead of making them is because you can become wealthier by going to work and using the money you earn to purchase the items you need.

In economics, this is called comparative advantage. Comparative advantage looks at what a party will lose by producing a certain item. In our example, your family lost a lot by producing its own clothes. They lost food, a house, furniture, electricity, water, etc. (assuming you did not trade for these other things). You, and the businesses you interact with, would be much better off trading your labor for money, which you can then use to trade for other things. This does not mean that the store is better at making clothes than you are. It simply means that

FREE TRADE MAKES BOTH SIDES BETTER OFF

they give up less (in terms of resources and time) in order to make the clothes than you do. The store probably gave up several thousand dollars for the batch of clothes that came in, while you gave up pretty much everything to make your own clothes.

This works on an international level between countries as well. Let's assume that country A can produce 10 cars and 20 boats in a given year, and it takes a half a year for each product to be produced. Country B can produce 10 cars and 16 boats in a given year (each product also takes a half a year, and both products are identical in each country). This means that each year, the two countries combined can produce 20 cars and 36 boats together, or 56 items total.

Now imagine if these countries were to trade based on comparative advantage. If country A were to only make cars, it would sacrifice 20 boats. If country B were to only make cars, it would sacrifice only 16 boats. Thus, country B has a comparative advantage over country A in making cars.

Now imagine, since country B has the comparative advantage in cars, country B only produces cars and country A only produces boats. Within one year, country A would produce 40 boats while country B produces 20 cars (since before, each country was diverting half a year to create each product). This means that the two countries have now created 20 cars and 40 boats for a total of 60 items. The number of total units produced from both countries is now larger. This means more money, products, and jobs in the overall economy. And since there are now more boats, prices on boats will likely drop, allowing more people to purchase boats.

When American jobs move overseas, the same things happen. Many of the countries that produce our goods have very few minimum wage laws, if any at all. Overseas companies are not required to provide health care if their workforce exceeds fifty people, either. Because of this, consumers in America get a cheaper product than they would otherwise, since companies are not forced to pay a higher price for labor, and people in other countries get a job. Both sides are better off.

However, it is—understandably—much easier to feel your neighbor's pain after a job loss than to see the effectively lower consumer prices that result from this exchange, so tariffs become popular. Tariffs are a very seductive policy, particularly to those who are patriotic. Tariffs promise that more jobs and money will stay in the country, so at first glance, it would seem idiotic *not* to use them. However, like other government actions, that is only at first glance.

Let's assume that a country puts a 10 percent tariff on oranges in order to help their orange farmers. This means that any orange that's imported from another country will cost 10 percent more, and that extra 10 percent will go to the government. This would, of course, discourage people from buying imported oranges, since they are more expensive, all the while attempting to push consumers toward domestically grown oranges. This is the same thing as putting a higher sales tax on a product from a certain company but not on the same product when it's made by another company simply because the first one is cheaper.

Because of this, all the people who live in the country levying the tariff will pay a higher price for something when they could have saved that 10 percent and put it toward something else. They could have put this money toward a different product, which would have created more jobs. Now the entire country must pay a higher price for breakfast because the orange farmers could not produce a better or cheaper product, and those who cannot afford the 10 percent increase are left without oranges. This policy also discourages the domestic farmers from creating a better product, because they are now protected by a 10 percent tax. The entire orange-consuming population is hurt because the orange farmers have been given special treatment by the government.

Tariffs are not the only form of protectionist policies. It's not uncommon for a certain company to receive some sort of benefit like a tax cut or free use of government land. This is also unfair, because it provides an advantage over other companies trying to compete within the company's industry. If one company in the construction industry is offered a tax cut in exchange for keeping their jobs at home, what happens to their competitors? Do those other construction companies get a tax cut too? What about the bar across the street that struggles just to keep the lights on? Do they also get a tax cut? It's possible that the reason the original construction company was going to move its jobs overseas is because their domestic competitors were running them out of business and they needed to find a way to somehow cut costs. It's possible that their competitors are simply better companies. Should the government really be holding the hand of the failing company?

When tariffs or any other protectionist policies are enacted in a country, the general population is oppressed with higher prices or an unfair, government-sanctioned disadvantage. I know it can be tempting to support such policies because you care about American workers, but whenever someone says, "The government should [do X]," you *should* be extremely skeptical.

There are ways to enjoy the benefits of free trade while keeping our jobs in America. If we would just begin to take chainsaws to the suffocating webs of red tape that paralyze our industries, cut taxes—by a lot—and end hurtful government mandates, businesses would decide to keep their jobs here. Many business owners love the United States as much as you and I, and would love nothing more than to grow jobs here, but big government leaves them with no choice if they are to keep their businesses afloat.

Building a factory in another country and hiring and training an entirely new workforce is neither cheap nor easy. It costs a lot of time and money to do, so there must be real reasons for a company to move. Those reasons are taxes, regulations, and mandates. Cut those and you will see job growth in America like never before.

QUICK-DRAW POINTS:

- Free trade makes both participants wealthier.

- A trade deficit is not always a bad thing. Most of us are in a trade deficit, as most of us did not build our own house, make our own clothes, grow our own food, build our own cars, pump our own oil out of the ground for those cars, etc.

- Tariffs hurt both trading partners, no matter which side implements one. The country that implements the tariff forces its people to pay a higher price for goods, and the country that is subject to the tariff will see a decrease in exports of the taxed good.

- If you want to keep jobs in America, decrease taxes and cut regulations and mandates. These are the only sorts of policies that will allow us to advance further and protect our interests.

9. ARE WE DESTROYING THE ENVIRONMENT?

One of the most popular arguments against capitalism is that consumers are destroying the earth. Proponents of this argument say that we are using too many resources, cutting down too many trees, killing all the fish, and throwing trash everywhere, all of which will eventually destroy entire ecosystems. Some of the big names in the environmental movement then proceed to board their private jet and fly to their next destination, where they will be paid hundreds of thousands of dollars for another speech on the evils of our destructive ways.

According to many ardent environmental activists, if you do not believe radical steps should be taken to reduce carbon emissions, you are a "climate change denier." They accuse "deniers" of not caring about the well being of the earth and insist that we will all be dead soon because of them. This is a bullying tactic that activists use in order to obscure the

ARE WE DESTROYING THE ENVIRONMENT?

fact that it simply is not feasible to stop emitting carbon at the moment.

In 2016, roughly 15 percent of the United States' energy came from renewable sources.[46] According to the U.S. Department of Energy, California produces a whopping 635,062 billion BTUs (a unit used to measure energy) from renewable energy each year.[47] The government of California has encouraged green energy through subsidies and regulations on nonrenewable energy sources. However, Californians are paying the true price—literally. It turns out that California's electricity rates are 50 percent higher than the national average.[48]

In its current state, renewable energy simply cannot sustain human consumption right now. Forcing it onto people has caused prices to skyrocket. Maybe many people in America, though burdened by it, might be able to afford a serious increase in energy rates. That's not to say that Texas would see the same 50 percent increase if it were to follow California, but it would surely see an increase of some sort. However, there are billions of people in the developing world that can barely afford enough fuel just to heat a can of beans once a week.[49] In reality, forcing a green energy policy onto these people as well would push them from desperation to death.

Let's pretend the United States were to completely stop using all nonrenewable energy sources today. On top of that, let's pretend that we didn't spend money on subsidies to increase our renewable energy capacity. If this scenario occurred, 15 percent of our energy consumption could be maintained—and 85 percent would be lost. Eventually people will want to eat, which requires cooking, which requires fuel. Since we would only be left with 15 percent of our usual energy supply, the prices for energy would go through the roof. People would be forced to burn any available fuel in order to cook, possibly including animal feces, which is actually more harmful to the environment and people's health than burning coal (it probably smells worse too).[50] The sad thing is that many people in developing countries only have animal feces to rely on as a source of fuel.

Capitalism has a simple answer to the pollution issue that does not push people into poverty: economic incentives. The very first solar panel ever created was not nearly as efficient as the ones we use today, and it was also a lot more expensive. What made them cheaper and more efficient? Mainly competition, which spurred technological advancements. Solar companies knew they needed to create a better, cheaper product to compete and make more money. So, they did.

Every scientist, entrepreneur, and inventor knows that whoever creates the machine or process that can deliver safe, renewable, and *cheap* energy on a mass scale will become one of the richest people in the world overnight. This is quite the incentive, and it is also why calculators used to be the size of an entire room but are now just another app on your phone. If the free market would just be given time to operate, we would soon figure out how to produce energy in a clean, cheap, and economically feasible way. Just think back to when humanity mainly used trains for mass transit. Each route would require a new railroad, which would take up precious space and land. Now we can simply use the sky to fly to any destination that has a usable runway. As with every technology, renewable energy will eventually grow to be economically feasible. But to force people to use it right now would devastate humanity.

Some say that we are depleting our resources. They say that our current resource supplies simply cannot sustain our massive human population growth in the future. Because of this, they say, we need to stop using nonrenewable energy sources and switch to renewable ones. We have already gone over the harm this would cause to humans, but what would happen if nonrenewable sources started to disappear more quickly than renewable ones could be harvested? As the nonrenewable sources began to shrink, the prices for these resources would rise, less people would use them as a result, and there would be even greater incentive to create a better way to collect renewable energy.

Another thing to point out is that we may not actually know all the possible uses for our natural resources yet. At one point in human history, oil was worthless. We did not know how to refine it, put it into an engine, mix it with oxygen, and add a spark in order to move a car. It is within the realm of possibility that we could figure out a way to use a currently "useless" resource for energy. Maybe something even more abundant than oil.

Another common criticism made by environmentalists is that we are cutting down all the trees, which are important for converting carbon dioxide into oxygen for humans. The problem with that accusation is that American logging companies replant trees once they cut them down. This is the same concept as a farmer reusing a plot of land. The farmer does not abandon his land after one harvest, and neither do loggers. This policy has worked so well, in fact, that we now have more trees in the United States than we did one hundred years ago.[51]

The real problem of deforestation comes from countries where forests are owned by the government. According to the World Bank, Venezuela's forests have been in sharp decline since 1990.[52] Keep in mind that Venezuela is a country with the world's largest oil reserves,[53] and yet its people are still starving. According to the same World Bank report, forest area has *increased* in the United States over the same time period.

The problem that countries such as Venezuela have with deforestation is called the tragedy of the commons. Imagine a field where sheep graze. The field is not owned by anyone, so grazing there is free. Naturally, many shepherds lead their sheep there to graze. Because nobody owns the field, nobody keeps it in good condition. This leads to overgrazing, and eventually the field cannot feed any sheep at all. If someone owned the field, they may charge a small fee for the shepherds to let their sheep graze. Some shepherds may not think the price is worth it, and will take their sheep elsewhere. Others would lead their sheep to the field to graze. Now that the owner of the field has an incentive to sustain the field, they will. The field will last much longer this way. You see, if there is no incentive to replant the trees in forests after logging, no trees will be replanted. When something is owned by the people as a whole, there is no real incentive for one individual to take care of that thing, like in the case of Venezuela's forests.

Fuel sources such as coal, oil, natural gas, and nuclear power have created a much better world for humans. We can now heat and cool our homes in areas of the world where the temperature drops below 0 degrees and breaks 100 degrees. We can now cook meals without chopping trees down from the backyard or using animal feces as fuel. We can now get to work in a climate-controlled vehicle rather than a horse and buggy. Not only can we order products from our desk chair, we can get our online orders within a few days because of fast air and ground travel.

It is true that a factory should not be allowed to pump toxic waste into a lake used by the neighboring town. This is not what ardent environmentalists are calling for. Many of them are calling for something that will utterly destroy many people.

Do not submit to the bullying tactics that label you some sort of monster if you do not believe carbon emissions should be forcibly rolled back. You are not a monster for wanting the whole world to survive while knowing that one day we *will* find a way to harvest unlimited renewable energy.

One final point. Former Vice President Al Gore is a staunch environmental activist and is known for his *An Inconvenient Truth* documentaries about global warming. However, Gore's home has, at times, consumed 34 times the amount of energy that the average American household uses. When he was called out about this seeming double standard, he pledged to make it right, spending $250,000 on renovations to make his home more green. The outcome? His home now produces enough green energy to run for twenty-one days every year before having to revert back to nonrenewable sources.[54] If the people telling you that we are going to destroy our planet if we do not change our evil ways are not changing their own evil ways, things are probably not as bad as they say.

QUICK-DRAW POINTS:

- Forcing the market to switch to another energy source will only hurt it. We hope that one day we will be able to rely on a clean source of energy that can sustain us, but it's simply not available right now. And the only way we will get there is through the free market inventing new ways to harness renewable energy.

ARE WE DESTROYING THE ENVIRONMENT?

- Many poor countries have a shortage of energy, and when the people in these countries do get some access to energy, it is not green energy. To force these people to give up what little energy resources they have would likely kill them.

- Oil was once useless and something of a nuisance. They don't call it "black gold" for nothing. It is possible that someday we will find a new source of energy that is even more abundant and clean than oil—but the only way to do this is through free-market inventors tinkering with possible energy sources.

- The people telling you to panic about our energy usage situation are not panicking, so should you be?

- Factories should not be allowed to pump their toxic waste into a public lake that is used by a neighboring town. However, this is not an excuse to ban fossil fuels outright.

10. PROFITS ARE NOT EVIL

Opponents of capitalism have a problem with profits. They like to claim that there is something inherently wrong with companies turning huge profits every year, and they love to point out when a company earns truckloads of cash while its minimum wage workers do not. But is this really an injustice? You probably know the answer by now.

It isn't wrong for a company to turn a huge profit for several reasons. The most important one is the fact that the company made the profit from people who willingly purchased their product or service. The company offered something that people wanted and were willing to give their money up for. The company never held customers at gunpoint forcing them into buying the product.

Most large companies have stockholders, investors, and owners. All three of these groups of people were betting on the company. When an owner bets their life savings on a crazy idea, they may fail. In fact, statistically, they most likely will. For them to come out on top after taking such a crazy risk when others did not is not an injustice. The injustice occurs when the government forcibly claims the company as their own in the name of equality, an event that happens frequently in socialist countries such as Venezuela. (This process is called "nationalization.") Likewise, the small-business owner who did not cut themselves a check for the first two years of their business's existence in order to make payroll every month did not perform an injustice.

When investors give money to a new company, they are taking a tremendous risk. Startup companies require a lot of capital, and that money does not come out of thin air. People offer their own money in exchange for a mere promise of returns (or, in some cases, other people's money—which arguably raises the risk for the creditor). So when this company finally does turn a profit—a rare occurrence—the investors are rewarded for their risk-taking.

As for shareholders, they make business decisions that can change the course of a company. For them to receive a cut of the profit that results from their prudent decision-making is not wrong, because they were responsible for generating the profit.

Each of these situations has another side to it. It's not like every business turns huge profits. Most fail, which means those who took a risk lost their investments, whether they be time, energy, or money.

If it were really possible to get rich by simply applying for the right to operate, everyone would be rich. Business is an extremely difficult venture. It requires months or even years of very little sleep, sacrifices that few are willing to make, tough decisions that can break someone, and other challenging hurdles. What's the incentive for making such a commitment to a project that may never even turn into a Fortune 500 company? Profit.

The only way to be profitable in a free market is to sell the best possible product at the lowest possible price. This is one of the first things anyone learns in an introductory economics class, if their professor is honest. Selling a poor product at the same price as a better product will run a company out of business. A good product at a higher price than similar alternatives will also run a company out of business. Companies are not committing thievery against you when a price tag is high. If they attempt thievery, you will run them out of business by consuming their rivals' offerings.

Some companies even wait years to turn a profit. It took Amazon a whole six years to turn a real profit.[55] Even a powerhouse company that most (if not all) of us have used did not earn a profit for a very long time. Business is very difficult, and when one turns a profit they should be congratulated rather than scorned.

Profits act as a catalyst for innovation. Humans have inarguably benefited from transportation innovation. But why does Boeing continue to improve their planes? In order to beat out their competitors and turn a profit for their investors and shareholders.

For many people there is a negative feeling attached to the word "profit." This may be because they believe that companies are turning huge profits while they are shelling out all of their hard-earned cash for the company's products. However, in 2015, the average profit margin for corporations in America was 7.5 percent. Despite this, survey-takers believed it to be 36 percent.[56] Clearly, there is a disconnect between what people believe companies are making and what they actually are making. This is why minimum wage hikes and mandates are fought so hard. Companies simply are not making the profits people believe they are. It can only be harder for small businesses in more competitive environments. This is why many shops end up just closing their doors after minimum wage hikes.

If a company could regularly turn a 36 percent profit margin, they would be able to poach every good worker in the country by offering much higher wages, more benefits, etc. No one would want to work for this company's competitors, creating a race to the top for wages and benefits because if the competitors did not respond with higher wages or better benefits, they would soon be out of business.

Profits decide what products survive in a free market. If a certain product doesn't create any profit, it will be dropped, because clearly not enough people wanted it. The only people hurt in this situation are the business owners who attempted to sell the unwanted product. However, in government-run economies, products can stick around even if there is no demand for them simply to pad fake employment numbers.

We discussed how thin profit margins can be—an average of 7.5 percent in 2015. Government actions that attack even these modest numbers will only bring companies down and push them out of business. Thousands of jobs could be lost and those people will be forced to turn to government aid. This is intentional. The new welfare recipients will demand higher tax rates on those working to cover the costs of this government spending. The higher taxes will push more businesses out, and the vicious cycle continues.

Lastly, it's worth pointing out that working for profits reduces waste. Nobody likes to see waste, but pursuing profits actually incentivizes companies to reduce waste as much as possible. This is because companies still have to pay for any wasted material they purchased in order to make their product. If a company makes aluminum rods, it's in their interest to use every last ounce of aluminum they purchased, and not just simply throw the leftover aluminum out after they hit a certain quota or profit point. You can see how this saves resources of all kinds. In a government-run economy, however, there is no profit incentive, so any government-run industry has no motivation to avoid waste, as doing so does not affect their bottom line. All they need to do is hit their quotas.

The stigma against profits is not a fair one.

PROFITS ARE NOT EVIL

There is no stigma against those who do not profit. However, someone who profits creates more wealth for the entire world to enjoy. The entire world gets in on these profits when the person who generated them purchases products or services. Most importantly, though, profits serve a very critical role in the economy. They ensure that people are given the products they want at a price that is fair. If a product is bad or a price is not fair, a lack of profits will punish the company selling that product.

QUICK-DRAW POINTS:

- Profits eliminate bad products from the market and keep good ones in it.

- Profits act as a reward for risked time, capital, and energy. Without them, nobody would risk their time, capital, or energy on creating the next hit product.

- Taken together, companies are not actually making thirty-six cents on every dollar you spend on their products. At the end of the day the real number is closer to seven or eight cents for every dollar.

- Profits drive efficiency. If a great product in all other respects is not efficient to make, it may lose money. This gives companies incentive not to waste material. This saves resources and is better for the environment over the long run. In a government-run economy, there is no worry about profit, and so there is no incentive to reduce waste.

11. COERCION VS. LIBERTY

One question to answer when considering a free market or a state-run economy is, "How do we want to live: under coercion or with liberty?" Every government regulation, rule, law, tax, and other act of control must be implemented with coercion—that is, force. If you do not pay your taxes, the government will show up and you will be tried for tax evasion. This is technically force. Not to say that all taxes are bad. For example, some are necessary to ensure public safety and national security. We need taxes in order to build a military that can defend our people. And when the government sets a speed limit, it uses the threat of a ticket or jail time to impose compliance. If you do not pay the ticket or if you try to leave jail before your time is up, you may be met by the end of a gun barrel. The point is, all government mandates are imposed by force at the end of the day. People are coerced into certain actions or inactions.

COERCION VS. LIBERTY

Liberty, on the other hand, is the idea that one is allowed to do whatever they wish as long as they do not hurt someone else in the process. Obviously, we need to include the last part of that phrase because we cannot allow serial killers to run around offing people with no repercussions. For example, you should be allowed to open that shop that you have always wanted to run, as long as you legally obtain the land and pay the contractor their price to build said shop. Neither people nor governments should be allowed to just take something that does not belong to them simply because they want it.

Big-government advocates assume that bureaucrats in Washington, D.C., know what is best for families in Midland, Texas. No matter what those families think, the government should have control over their lives. The free market, however, does not allow for such servitude. In the free market, what is yours is yours and what is someone else's is theirs. The ideological war between the free market and a state-run economy is not truly a war of economics. It is truly, at its core, a war over people's individuality and liberties.

Here's an example. Advocates of the government-run economy attempt to hold the lie that everyone will be able to have the occupation they want in their utopia. For example, Nancy Pelosi once said, "Think of an economy where people could be an artist or a photographer or a writer without worrying about keeping their day job." It would be wonderful if artists of all kinds could live comfortably off of their creations, but the truth is that there is just not as much demand for nice paintings as there is for food. Accordingly, in a market-based economy such as the United States, employment in agriculture dwarfs employment in the visual arts. This is because people need to eat, and the food industry has developed to meet this national demand.

In a government-run economy, however, there is no incentive to meet demand, because producers are only accountable to the government, not the population. In a society where anyone who wants to be an artist (or anything else) can be—that is, a society where jobs are totally divorced from demand—why would anyone want to do the hard work of growing food? Most likely, they wouldn't. But in a market-based economy, the people who do the hard work are rewarded for their labor. And those who want to take a risk to be that next great painter, can. Rather than being subject to whatever job the government thinks they ought to fulfill.

The problem with an economy untethered to demand was well known in the Soviet Union: shortages. The Soviet Union was riddled with shortages. Food, cars, clothing, anything you can think of—it all had a waiting period. People would stand in lines for hours to get food for their families, and in many cases, everything was sold out by the time they got to the front of the line. There was no bread, milk, or cheese: simple things that we take for granted in the United States. In the United States, we complain when two people are ahead of us in the checkout line; meanwhile, the shelves behind us are stocked with about twenty different types of bread, milk, and cheese.

I bring this up because if the government is to satisfy the demand for food, some of those artists, photographers, and writers that Pelosi mentioned will have to become farmers or ranchers. The government will have to force them into these businesses. Not because they want to be in these businesses, but because in a state-run economy, they have to. (Also, speaking of musicians, keep in mind that they are frequently executed in North Korea.) Here in the United States, you can be a musician if you want, and if you are a superstar, you'll become rich because of it. But it will be a result of the demand for your music.

Also, the Soviet Union had "free" health care. Nancy Pelosi's dream—or at least an extreme version of it—has already taken its course in human history, and it was a nightmare for the people of the Soviet Union. Every person was covered, but naturally, like we discussed earlier, nobody had any choice anymore. The good doctors left the field, as there was no more incentive to cure people, and the government told patients where they could and could not go for treatment. The new doctors were given little pay and forced to treat vast numbers of people every day.[57] Just like they had to do with food, the government eventually had to ration health care and demand was not satisfied. This led to shortages and extremely poor health-care quality. But those on the top, many times, cannot feel this strife themselves because the people pay for their lifestyles. So, they continue to bang this drum because they themselves are not subject to its effects and it usually always wins votes in the beginning.

Another point to consider is the fact that big government, inevitably intoxicated by its own power and commitment to keeping that power, will censor art and speech. The artist, photographer, and writer will not be able to create what they want, but instead what the government tells them to. Evil governments like the Soviet government and the Nazi government censored any work that could be seen as dissenting against the ruling regime. This would, of course, mean that these artists are no longer artists. They no longer have the liberty to create what they see fit, but must produce what the government says they can; they are propagandists. If an artist wants to depict the rampant starvation spreading throughout their country, they cannot. Instead, they would be forced to depict something patriotic in order to make a hellhole look like Heaven. In the United States, you can paint a picture expressing dissent toward the president and not fear the Secret Service knocking on your door. You might upset the other half of the country, though. Which is what is so great about America: you can do something that half

COERCION VS. LIBERTY

the country may hate and you still have the right to do it—and they still have the right to hate it.

At the core of their ideology, true tyrants have one thought. They think that you are too stupid, and thus incapable, of running your own life, so they must. They must provide your health care, your income, your car, your food, and everything else a person might want or need. They think that the people as a whole are not nearly as smart as a single one of them. This is what makes their ideology such a power grab. In reality, the opposite is true. You know much better than them when it comes to living your life, and you are also extremely capable.

Communism, socialism, democratic socialism, or whatever label people want to put on it today all mean the same thing in the end. They mean the people will be forced to act in a certain way, eat a certain amount of food, work a certain job, and the like. Capitalism and the free market allow people to make these choices for themselves. In a free market you have the choice to gorge yourself and gain weight or exercise and stay thin. You can choose your occupation, car, home, and dreams.

Imagine a young person in a free market. They can choose to do or be whatever they want. If they want to start the next Apple, it will not be easy, but it can be done. If they want to become a police officer, training will be no cakewalk, but they can do that as well. If they want to become a surgeon, they can do that, too. Now place that person in a communist environment. If this person is male, he will most likely be drafted into the military when he reaches the proper age. If he does not stay in the military his whole life, he can move into a different sector that the government deems acceptable, like mining, science, or logging; it all depends on where the government thinks he ought to be. He can no longer be a doctor like he wanted. His potential contributions will never be fulfilled. Maybe he was the person that was going to find the cure for cancer; now, the world is that much less well off. There is no freedom in a state-run economy, and to trade freedom for job security in a state run-economy is to endorse voluntary slavery.

Now imagine two people in a state-run economy. They both receive the same coupons/stamps for various goods like food and clothing. Imagine that one of them prefers to have dinners with many vegetables and a healthy balance of meat while the other only likes to eat meat. You can see how these people's preferences would come into conflict in a rationed food system. The first person may not be able to get as many vegetables as they would like, and the second person wouldn't have enough meat. They both don't have any choice, however. As a natural result, people put in such a situation would begin trading coupons/stamps in order to get what they prefer. This would, ironically, create an underground free market, or black market, where certain vouchers/stamps are worth more and some are worth less.

COERCION VS. LIBERTY

This actually happened in the Soviet Union: coupons effectively functioned as cash and people would trade them for what they wanted. Even in state-run economies, capitalism finds a way.

This time, imagine the same two people in a free market. For example's sake, let us assume that they have the same job, and thus, the same income. Now the first person can spend the money they choose on the vegetables they want and the second person can spend whatever they want on meat. Are they being subjected to the preferences of a bureaucrat in Washington? No. Both individuals are allowed to choose how they spend their income in a just society.

"Spending their income how they see fit" does not mean taking their income in the form of taxes and then spending it on programs that that person may not even support. Here's a quick example. Let's pretend that a local government takes X number of dollars from its city residents, in the form of taxes, in order to fund a public housing project. Now, with that X amount of money, one house is built, and one family moves in on someone else's dollar. Imagine now that the people who were taxed wanted to fund a new local business with that money. That business would have created at least a few jobs, one of which might have gone to a family member living in public housing—thereby enabling that family member to apply for a mortgage. Also, the local area is now left without a new, life-bettering product or service from that business. Those entrepreneurs that were looking for funding are now left out in the cold as well.

The same is true for individuals. Imagine you are taxed $10,000 every year. Those taxes might go to a multitude of things, but the fact is you no longer have that $10,000. That $10,000 could have been a down payment on a beautiful new car, paid off your debts, or maybe even put your child through private school. The point is that you no longer have control over the money that you worked for.

You might have a lot in common with your best friend, but you probably do not have everything in common with them. Likewise, the whole country certainly does not align on every preference. However, in a state-run economy, your choices are chosen by the leader. If they like chocolate ice cream, so do you. If they like a certain cereal, so do you. Because those will be the only options in the supermarket—if you are lucky enough to get there in time before the place is raided and nothing is left.

The idea of artists and photographers not worrying about their day job is a nice one, and we wish aspiring artists and photographers the best. However, what artists get paid? The ones that create something that people are willing to pay for. If an artist creates art that nobody likes but is still being paid for it, someone is being wronged. Someone is being forced to pay for that art even though they wouldn't have if they had the choice. Your favorite musician or band is not subsidized; they survive and continue to create music because you are willing to pay the price to consume their music. In that same vein, you are not forced to pay for terrible music or even music you do not like but others consider good. Not everyone is a fan of modern pop music, but not everyone needs to pay for it. And even though not everyone pays for it, it survives because there are enough people who willingly do pay for it.

When the government subsidizes Tesla by offering tax credits for purchasing one of their cars for personal use, someone is still being wronged. That tax revenue is lost, which must be covered by someone else now, but what about Dodge? How does Dodge feel about the fact that the government gives discounts for buying someone else's car just because the government thinks they should drive that sort of car? Dodge then loses sales due to this policy. If the government isn't careful, it can run car companies like Dodge out of business until only Tesla is left. But this is the point of socialism: to control the means of production. And once the government has the auto industry in their pocket, they can move on to other industries.

If you come up with some crazy idea for a new type of shirt that people may love, you can pursue that in a free market. People might even eat it up and make you rich. Or they might hate it and you will have to try a new idea. However, in a state-run economy weighed down by bureaucracy you'd be hard-pressed to even get approval to produce the shirt before you died of old age. Even if you were able to somehow get to the right department, you would probably be denied on the grounds that, say, we need more farmers. Not to mention the fact that you probably had to skip many days of work in order to push this idea, so now you're probably in jail for never showing up to work. Even if you were able to somehow get this shirt produced in a government run economy, the government would own your profits.

The debate over big or limited government is not truly about equality, GDP growth, or jobs. At its core, it is an argument between control or freedom. What the government wants or your dreams. Coercion or liberty.

QUICK-DRAW POINTS:

- The debate over which major economic system we should adopt can be boiled down to one question: Do we want liberty or coercion in our economic system? While a government-run economy, by definition, requires force, free markets offer the liberty to choose one's own path and the amount of work one wishes to put in. And, it offers rewards for selling or producing a better product.

- Turning things like health care over to the government gives it the right to dictate what people consume in the name of saving money.

- In a government-run economy operating on a coupon system, choice is lost. You only get so many coupons for bread, so if you want more bread than the average person, the only option is to trade other coupons for more bread coupons. In a free market you spend your money on what you want, not what someone else thinks you need.

- If you want to take a big risk to make it big in a free market, you can do that. There is no risk and reward in a government-run economy.

- In a free market, you choose your path in life. In a government-run economy, the government chooses your path in life.

12. INDEPENDENCE, PERSONAL RESPONSIBILITY, AND THE WELFARE STATE

Ronald Reagan was correct when he said, "Welfare's purpose should be to eliminate, as far as possible, the need for its own existence." However, the use of welfare has only grown over the years since its implementation.[58] Obviously, there have been spikes during challenging economic times, but the overall picture is that use is on the rise. This is no mistake. The easiest way for a government to gain total control over its people is to strip them of their sense of independence. As more people enter the welfare system, more people become dependent on the state for food, housing, clothing, etc.

This becomes a vicious cycle. When people depend on the government for their basic needs, someone is going to have to foot that bill. Taxes will need to be raised in order to cover new expenses, and these new taxes will cause more people to fall into government dependence—which will in turn require a rise in taxes. Eventually, the government will need to put these people to work by taking over the economy and any remaining private assets will be seized from honest people.

Our welfare system was created in response to the Great Depression. But we have been out of the Depression for a very long time, so why is it still hanging around? This is because subsidies are very easy to give. It's not hard to convince someone to accept something for free, but it is very difficult to stop a subsidy. In other words, while it's very easy to convince someone on welfare to vote for an increase in the amount of allotted welfare, it is very difficult to convince the same person to vote to end welfare.

This is why it would be so difficult to generate the support to end other programs, such as Social Security or Medicare, if a politician were to try to do so. It's also why it is so very easy to grow these sorts of programs: people like free stuff, and they do not like to give up the free stuff that they get every year. This is just human nature, and it gives those who want to expand government a real edge. This is why if governments are not kept in check, they can very easily grow to the point where they are crushed under their own weight, like the Soviet Union was.

The Soviet Union did not fall because of the mean old Americans. The country that killed its own people by the millions fell because the welfare state simply could not sustain itself any longer. The only thing the American government really had to do to spur this collapse was to make it a death sentence to attack us militarily, and then wait for the Soviet system to fail. Both countries admittedly spent massive amount of money on their militaries, but only one didn't implode.

There were vast differences between the two countries during this time. In the United States, many families owned more than one car, while in the Soviet Union families were lucky if they had even one. In the United States, the middle class was well fed, but in the Soviet Union there were food shortages (and no middle class). It's not as though the American people were somehow naturally more productive than the Soviets. The difference was that one was a welfare state run by the government and the other had a populace with liberty.

A true welfare state leaves its people with no option but to stay in the welfare system. This is because welfare states eventually wrap the economy so tightly that there is no way for a person to break free and become self-sufficient. Fail in a welfare state, and you will more than likely still be stuck in the welfare system. At least in a free market, if you fail at something, you can start again the next day, or even switch to a new industry. In a free market you are never stripped of your independence. Michael Jordan's famous quote, "I've failed over and over and over again in my life. And that is why I succeed," would not make any sense in a welfare state, as it is purely defined.[59] In a welfare state, when one falls,

INDEPENDENCE, PERSONAL RESPONSIBILITY, AND THE WELFARE STATE

they stay down. There is no reason to get up again and face the humiliation of the fall when someone else is putting food on the table.

That's not to say we do not need some sort of basic safety net, but that safety net should be constructed more as a trampoline than a spider web. In other words, when someone falls into the net, they should rise up again instead of sticking there. The fact that a) our safety net is increasingly being used; and b) children of parents on welfare are much more likely to be on it than children whose parents did not accept welfare show that it is not propelling people to independence.[60]

This problem could arise from a variety of issues, but in reality it is probably a mix of the following ones. First, government mandates put a huge strain on businesses, which can hinder their ability to expand and hire more employees. For example, the Obamacare mandate that forced all businesses with fifty or more employees to pay for the health care of their full-time employees hindered many small businesses from expanding, and probably forced many already over the fifty-employee mark to contract.

Cutting regulations would also open new doors to employment. When a company has to spend time and energy on tiptoeing around regulations, they lose production potential. If this potential could be tapped, there would be a demand for more employees.

Second, high taxes, which are eventually used to

support the safety net (ironically enough), also hinder job openings. As we discussed, businesses are not turning ungodly profits after taxes. On the contrary, many are lucky to be in the black in a given year. When they have more leeway with their budget, businesses will use that extra cash to compete better with their rivals. This means jobs. Maybe they use the cash to research new products, survey their market, or even produce more goods. All of these things require manpower, and thus, more employees.

In addition to mandates and taxes, minimum wage laws prevent people from working jobs whose value is not equivalent to (or above) the minimum wage. When a wage is forcibly raised over what it is worth in terms of production value, businesses close, employees are laid off, and machines take their jobs. These results will cause more people to fall into the spider web-style safety net.

Finally, welfare measures directed at people who have the means to reenter the labor force should be uncomfortable. Of course, we do not want people to starve while they are on it, but it should be uncomfortable enough to make people want to enter the labor force again. In other words, welfare should not make people content. But we should not implement this policy without first making the aforementioned changes to regulations, mandates, and taxes. If we were to make welfare uncomfortable before freeing up the market, people would probably try to escape the safety net but would have fewer opportunities to do so. The goal of welfare should be to get as many people back into the workforce as possible.

In a perfect world, there would be no need for a welfare system. Communities, families, churches, and other groups would fill in the gaps of the free market when someone falls through. However, this is hard for them to do when the American people keep less of their money after taxes and while the economy is bound in red tape.

A study conducted by the Brookings Institution shows that in order to avoid poverty in America, all someone needs to do is wait until they are twenty-one to get married, not have kids before marriage, graduate high school, and enter into a full-time job. Doing this gives anyone a 2 percent chance of falling into permanent poverty and nearly a 75 percent chance of entering the middle class.[61] These are great odds, and the conditions required to get those odds are within the grasp of any American, no matter what anyone says.

No voter, on the American Right or Left, likes the idea of a country where there are a few, rich elites with the rest of the population in poverty. If there is anything that voters can agree on, it is that we need to expand the middle class and shrink the number of people in poverty. However, we cannot do this if we are disincentivizing people from joining the middle class, and especially not if we are making it harder to remain in the middle class.

Liberty was the core value of American independence: religious liberty, liberty from taxes that were not agreed to, and liberty from British tyranny. Along with liberty comes independence. We did not fight to be dependent on the state. We fought to be self-sufficient and to have the ability to make decisions for ourselves. These are the values that primed the United States to one day become the world's premier superpower.

America will not always be the world's superpower just by divine right. Britain was, at one point, the world's superpower. America's core, foundational values are what made it what it is today, and they are also the only values that will keep the country in its current position. We need to encourage independence rather than construct a welfare state. Because without our independence, then what do we even have? Without it, we are owned by someone else just because they sit in a government building.

Along the lines of independence comes personal responsibility. Personal responsibility should be something we encourage for the simple fact that someone should not be negatively affected by the decisions or actions of someone else. For example, you would not intentionally throw someone in prison for a murder they did not commit. Likewise, we should not condone forcing someone to pay someone else's doctor bills because they lived an unhealthy lifestyle and require a lot of expensive medical care.

Each person should reap the consequences of their decisions whether they are good or bad. This is because as we learn to keep doing the good things and stop doing the bad things, humanity as a whole will improve. Instead of a society where everyone relies on someone else to survive, we could achieve a society where everyone is self-sufficient.

Let me provide an example from my own experience. A couple years ago, I walked into a fast-food restaurant just as the line had cleared. As I walked up to the counter, the cashier pulled out his phone and started using it. He never looked up to greet me or even ask what I wanted to order. Intrigued, I waited and watched to see just how long it would take him to finish his business on company time. I even cleared my throat because, you know, he may not have noticed my presence, but I never interjected. I don't know how long it truly was, but after what felt like several minutes, an older, heavyset man—who was not nearly as amused as I— got into line behind me. Once he realized what was going on, he proceeded to reprimand the cashier for texting at work.

This story teaches us a very important lesson. That cashier's actions behind the counter are the reason he was just the cashier and not the manager. No business owner in their right mind would promote that person; frankly, I don't even know how he still had a job at that point. The cashier's actions will reap negative consequences, and it would be wrong to force the man behind me in line to pay for those consequences in any way. Even after this brief encounter, there was a price to be paid. I never went back to that particular restaurant, and I can guarantee that the man behind me never went back, either. If this behavior were to happen often enough, the restaurant would lose all of its patrons, the owner would lose a business, and the cashier and his coworkers would all lose their jobs.

Personal responsibility is at the pinnacle of a free market. It will reward those who do a good job and refrain from rewarding those who do not.

QUICK-DRAW POINTS:

- The welfare state seduces people into becoming dependent on the state. In my opinion, this is an abomination. Humans should be free and independent.

- Welfare should act more as a trampoline that bounces people back into the workforce rather than a spider web that catches and holds them.

- In a perfect world, private citizens would be our welfare system. Organizations and individuals of all kinds would help lift people up from a rough patch or life crisis.

13. SELF-ENHANCEMENT

One of the greatest privileges of being human is the ability to better oneself. Everyone is born with a different subset of skills and abilities, but we all can improve these skills through practice. Professional athletes did not walk out of the womb ready to compete, and even someone who was not born with a natural skill can learn. We know that in a free market, people are pushed to better themselves because there are real, tangible benefits to doing so. A better salesman earns a higher commission, and the best managers can one day reach the C-suite. But not only does self-betterment help the person improving themselves, it also helps humanity as a whole, as people working toward self-improvement invent better products, draft better business models, or outperform expectations in a field. It should come as no surprise, though, that big-government policies can thwart the human desire and incentive to improve one's station.

In a communist society, people are given quotas to fulfill within a set time period. There is no incentive to produce more than this quota, and there is also no incentive to maintain a certain level of quality, since one unit is equal to one unit as far as the quota is concerned, despite whether it is good or poor in quality. For example, a baker in a communist society may be required to produce twelve loaves of bread every day. The baker will produce twelve loaves of normal bread every day. Trying to make the loaves tastier, or producing thirteen loaves instead of twelve, will not net the baker any increased reward since the government pays them according to their quota. Thus, there is no reason for the baker to work harder. In fact, it would be illogical for them to do so. Spending hours, days, or even years on a better recipe would be a waste of time and energy for the baker in this case. Because of this, there is an overall net loss for the baker and the people of his country.

Additionally, in state-run economies like the Soviet Union, the quota system had serious negative consequences for consumers. Soviet factories often released defective products simply to meet their quotas.[62] And, when products were overproduced, they were often wasted and basically thrown in the garbage. All this, despite the fact that there were shortages of various goods in these countries.

Another way communism thwarts the desire to improve oneself is through taxes. Of course, in a completely communist society, everyone's tax rate is

SELF-ENHANCEMENT

technically 100 percent, and the government distributes this stolen wealth how it sees fit. Let's see how this works. Suppose, for example, that everyone is given $1,000 every week from the government. The baker is not going to produce a better quality or higher quantity of bread, because they will not receive a bigger paycheck for their trouble. Without the hope of getting a bigger check, there is no reason to go the extra mile in order to improve. However, in a free market, the baker has an incentive to create a better product and beat out their competitors. That incentive is a bigger paycheck and eventually, the ability to hire workers to bake the bread in their bakery.

In a free market, one would be paid more, or given a promotion, for performing above average. Businesses, no matter the size, crave talent. They are willing to bend over backwards if it means acquiring the best prospective employee for the job. This is because the biggest consideration (if not the only consideration) any business has when hiring someone is how much money they will bring to the business. We see this when baseball teams compete with each other by offering huge salaries to ace pitchers or unstoppable batters. The free market has rightly rewarded these players for making themselves better than the rest of the field. Anyone who betters themselves in a capitalist society is usually rewarded in more ways than one, not just monetarily. Self-satisfaction is another reward that comes from bettering oneself. Arguably, this can hold even more value than more zeros in a bank account.

In a socialist or communist society, where the government owns all of the means of production, we run into a similar problem. Inventors are no longer incentivized to invent, because whatever they create is no longer theirs if it ever reaches the market. This could be a new form of energy, a car engine that runs on water, or a fertilizer that could feed the world. The hours of blood, sweat, and tears are not rewarded. Instead, the invention or idea is now owned by the government, which takes all of the rewards and gives them to other people who did not conceive or work on the project.

Socialism also kills the entrepreneurial spirit. Steve Jobs said that customers do not know what they want until they are shown what they want. If businesses are owned by the government, entrepreneurs no longer have an incentive to create the next iPhone. Nobody has any incentive to take a developing technology to the next level, because their idea will be stolen from them after it is born. Thus any time pure socialism is introduced into a country's economy, the country becomes stuck with the technology that it currently has. The same is true, of course, for communism. This is why the Soviet Union had the Lada while the rest of the world had Mercedes, Chevrolet, BMW, Ford, and so on. There were many more options in the free market, and these options all outmatched the quality and availability of the Lada.

SELF-ENHANCEMENT

Humans have a predisposition to create and to better themselves. This is the reason dogs did not invent the wheel, and dolphins did not invent the airplane. Religious folks may attribute this phenomenon to our souls calling us to a higher purpose, while atheists may attribute it to our heightened intelligence. Whatever you believe the source to be, it is the reason that humans have made such tremendous strides in self-improvement, while other animals have not. It is why we went from living in caves and making fire from brush and flint to living in homes with climate control and gas stoves. To punish, slow, or stop this march of human improvement with big-government policies will only keep humanity in its current state with no hope of advancement—that is, if it doesn't set us further back.

As explained, capitalism encourages self-betterment and creation. When the baker tries new recipe variations to make better bread, they are rewarded with more customers and a higher profit, which they are allowed to keep and use how they see fit. This may lead to more jobs, a new business, or a charitable donation. When the young doctor reads more books on medicine and tries new techniques, they are rewarded with an increased success rate and happier patients, which brings more patients in. When more patients come in sick and leave healed, it is better for both the doctor and the patients, and it also helps make a healthier world. This is not evil. In fact, this is a good thing for all of humanity. Capitalism enables people to keep the fruits of their labor and use them how they see fit. Thus, there is incentive to become better at whatever it is someone does. So not only do the lives of the baker and the doctor who chose to better themselves improve, but the lives of everyone influenced by their products or services improve as well.

QUICK-DRAW POINTS:

- Human improvement is most successfully cultivated through free markets, because in such a system the rewards for bettering oneself, at whatever task, are much greater.

- When there is no incentive to become better at something, which is what happens in a government-run economy, people will not put in the time or effort in order to do so. This results in a lower quality of care in hospitals, smaller crop yields, and decreased production overall.

- When the baker is not rewarded for baking better bread, they will not. The whole community is worse off for it.

14. VENEZUELA AND THE TALE OF TWO KOREAS

In a post on his website in 2011, Bernie Sanders seemed to endorse the view that Venezuela is one place where someone is more apt to find the American dream than America itself.[63] But socialism has not fared well in Venezuela, and the country has fallen into the same condition that other socialist states inevitably have. What was once South America's wealthiest country is now struggling to stay afloat.[64]

Venezuela is the most oil-rich country in the world,[65] but its people are still starving.[66] The reason for this counterintuitive result? Socialism. Since the avowed socialist Hugo Chavez came to power, in 1999, the Venezuelan government has been seizing private firms.[67] They justify this practice with a multitude of excuses. Regardless, with government ownership of the means of production comes no incentive to create more efficient means of production. The only incentive the government has to feed its people is to keep them from rising up and taking back what is rightfully theirs.

When a government seizes a private business, it does not just send a negative shockwave through the economy, as we discussed. It is signaling that the government is free to steal all the hours of labor and initial risks the owner took as though they mean nothing. The only crime the business owner committed was trying to sell something.

Though communism and socialism are two different systems of government, they do have two major similarities. The first is that they both have very massive central governments. The second is that they have, throughout history, ended up bringing massive amounts of death and suffering to their own people.

Violent protests in Venezuela in 2017 alone have led to the killing and imprisonment of many citizens. If it were true that the American dream is more easily found in a place like Venezuela, then why would there be such a need to put down rioters with force?

Food prices in the country have soared to unbelievable new highs. Some kitchen items that many Americans would take for granted like maple syrup can only be bought with a whole month's worth of minimum-wage salary. Not only that, but things like shampoos and deodorants are nowhere to be found.[68]

Shortages have riddled the country, and citizens must wait several hours just to get into a supermarket that may be sold out of items that they probably can't even afford.[69] This comes as no surprise, as we know that competition creates better quality and cheaper products. However, when the government owns all of the businesses, it has no competition. This leads to situations like the current one in Venezuela. Because when you don't need to compete to stay on top, you aren't going to put in much effort to stay there.

Socialism and communism both claim to fight for the working person—the common person. But time and time again, they plunge the entire populace into suffering. Whether or not these economic and political figures *intend* to do the right thing does not matter; they should be held accountable for their outcomes, just like when a drunk driver causes an accident that kills someone else. They may have never *intended* to cause an accident that killed someone else, but it doesn't matter. They must be held responsible.

When government fails people, many call for even more government. We saw this when Obamacare failed the American people. Premiums went up and people could not keep their preferred doctors as promised. However, many politicians blamed it on the fact that Obamacare just did not go far enough. We needed more regulations and mandates, they argued. We needed more government. This will only exacerbate the problems. In the case of Venezuela, we will not see the country begin to improve unless their politics take an about-face and march toward liberty rather than away from it.

Half a world away from Venezuela, the Korean Peninsula also offers a telling example. The two Koreas make for a prime comparison between the two major economic ideologies of our time—that is, free markets and state-run markets. This is because they share similar landmasses located in the same part of the world, the same race of people, and similar cultures. The only real difference—though it is a critical one—is that at their conception one country was propped up by Communist China and the other was propped up by the capitalist United States.

The results of these different paths speak for themselves. The GDP of South Korea is roughly thirty-seven times as large as North Korea's. GDP per capita in South Korea is $33,200—and $1,800 in North Korea. North Korea has half the population of South Korea, and their life expectancy is also ten years lower than their neighbor's.[70]

Not only would you be poor living in North Korea, you might end up a slave, or even executed. North Korea is known for its extensive use of sex and labor slaves alike. They are also known to execute musicians.[71] In South Korea, slavery is illegal, and the country has its own popular music artists.

If you view the Korean Peninsula from space at night, South Korea is lit up with lights, but North Korea is completely dark except, of course, for leader Kim Jong Un's home city, Pyongyang. And this is not because North Koreans are concerned about the environment. They simply do not have, or cannot afford, electricity. This is an extreme example of what is happening in California because of out-of-control energy prices, which is one reason why California's middle class is fleeing to Middle America. The rich can afford to pay the price while the poor cannot afford to get out of the state. The middle class, however, is searching for a new opportunity in places like the great state of Texas.

North Korea spends vast amounts of money and time on improving its military even though its people are starving. This is because the North Korean people do not have a say in the budget. If North Korea were an open democracy, and not a brutal communist dictatorship, it would probably be much less likely to saber rattle.[72] I believe that people, when given the choice, will always choose to be peaceful rather than go to war. This is why, when North Korea constantly threatens to nuke the United States, South Korea, or Japan, the South Korean people don't respond directly via the military, choosing instead to focus their energy on surviving another night.

Keep in mind that North Korea's official name is the Democratic People's Republic of Korea. So, just because someone puts the word "Democratic" in front of "Socialism" does not mean it will bring about a democratic outcome.

QUICK-DRAW POINTS:

- The people of the supposedly kind and compassionate socialist state of Venezuela are starving. Basic household items are next to impossible to find, and a whole month's salary can buy most people a bottle of maple syrup.

- The North and South Korean people are the same in every respect except for the governments they live under. While the North Koreans are malnourished, poor, and oppressed, the South Koreans have stocked supermarkets, their own Times Square, and the freedom to choose the life path they desire.

- North Korea is constantly threatening major world players with war. The South Korean government just wants to live and let live.

15. THE NEED FOR THE RIGHT CULTURE

A purely libertarian society will not serve itself well without a fulfilling culture with good and productive morals. Liberty is the vine; culture is the stake. If you have a strong culture that values hard work, personal responsibility, and community, liberty will have an easier time reaching its potential.

According to social psychologist Jonathan Haidt, conservatives are much more concerned with the idea of community.[73] This makes sense, as the small American towns where everyone knows each other are overwhelmingly conservative. They take care of each other, and when someone falls, the community is there to pick them up. They also tend to be very religious. This is not to say that religion is a requirement for a good culture, but the two are strongly correlated.

In a free-market society, there will inevitably be some people who fall through the cracks. Jobs may be lost, devastating illnesses may occur, and natural disasters may destroy entire towns. This is where the community needs to step in, and they will be much more prepared to do so if the government isn't cleaning them out every April.

This community involvement is in line with the conservative/libertarian idea of treating people as individuals rather than numbers and/or representatives of a particular race, gender, or ideology. This idea of treating each other like fellow Americans—again, rather than as part of a particular identity group—will fill in the cracks of the free market in a much quicker and more efficient manner than the government ever could.

Why is it faster and more efficient? Well, it is faster because there are no bureaucracies standing between you and your neighbor. But trusting the government to get a job done on time is another story (DMV anyone?). It is more efficient because it is case-specific rather than all-encompassing, like a blanket health-care policy that covers everything for everyone and would cost an inconceivable amount of money. In a free market, each illness would be handled on the individual level, which means there would be no grey area or spillover into a mandated procedure or test that would otherwise be useless.

Churches and other places of worship can also be a great gap filler. There is a plethora of places of worship—for many different religions—that would love to help someone out, even if they are a stranger. This

THE NEED FOR THE RIGHT CULTURE

idea of filling in the gaps does not end with the local community, though. Nonprofit organizations and charities can be an excellent gap filler for those who may fall through. The United Sates was founded on Judeo-Christian values. These values have served us well over the years, but this is not to say that they are the only good values in the world. For example, Japan does not have Judeo-Christian roots, but they have done quite well for themselves over the years as well.

We should agree on some basic values within our culture. In my opinion, those values are: what's mine is mine, what's yours is yours, don't try to force someone into acting a certain way, and nobody should try to force certain actions on you either. When someone falls and we have the ability to pick them up, we should. Not because of coercion, but because we are good people.

It is my belief that most people are good people. I realize, however, that a lot of other people do not feel this way. Not too long ago, I was in a class where we did a lot of group activities. I remember being curious, so I asked everyone if they thought that people were naturally good- or bad-natured. The two liberals said that people were, on average, bad, while the two conservatives and one libertarian said that people were good. Now this is no psychological study deserving of a Nobel Prize, but it can be quite telling when you think about it.

Living in a country where people have more freedoms requires a bit of trust from the population as a whole. You wouldn't want to live in a place like that if you thought everyone was a bad person. The liberals in the group probably just did not trust individuals to pick those who fell through the gaps up, while the conservatives (and libertarian) simply assumed this would be the case. It should come as no surprise then that even though conservatives make less money, they give more to charity.[74]

The sort of culture where people are willing to give through their own agency is what we need. Not only is this required to help those who have fallen, it is required for things like business loans. If an investor does not give an entrepreneur a chance with their money, we may miss out on a great new product. We need a culture where we can trust each other. I don't care what the world looks like right now; I still believe that most people are simply good. It's just that fringe population that always makes humanity look bad as a whole.

Our culture should also encourage personal responsibility. The identity politics movement of the Left, however, has turned this discussion into a war over who is more victimized. Yes, the United States has seen some horrible deeds committed within its lands, slavery being the most obvious. But that was in the past. Today, a middle-class farmer who may have some sort of family connection to a past slave owner should not be punished for it.

In my opinion, the important thing is what people are doing *now*. If someone is a blatant racist (and no, wanting a wall to secure your border is not racist), they should be shunned by we the people. However, that farmer is not a slave owner. They are just trying to feed their family in an honest way, and should not be demonized for the sins of their forefathers.

If we encourage personal responsibility rather than victimization, people will begin to break away and succeed. But if we only encourage people to think that someone is always out to get them—this invisible institutional force that nobody can track but is keeping them down—they will begin to believe it. When people believe that they are destined for failure, they will lose hope and feel no reason to get better or take responsibility for themselves.

Imagine a criminal thrown in prison for holding up a store at gunpoint. If this person is constantly told that the reason they are in prison is because the system at large hates them, and they wind up believing this, can you blame them? Then, once they get out of prison, how likely do you think they will be to commit another crime? Now imagine if personal responsibility was taught. There would be a different outcome.

Personal responsibility helps avoid the problem of always casting blame on someone else. When a team loses a game, was it the ref's fault? Or was it just that they were not good enough to beat the other team? Maybe it was the other team's fault for being too good? If a team believes this, what reason do they have to hit the film room the next day? None, really; because it was someone else's fault that they lost, they have no incentive to get better.

As mentioned before, waiting to get married until you are twenty-one, waiting to have children until marriage, graduating high school, and getting a full-time job drops your chance of being permanently poor to just 2 percent. It also gives you a 75 percent chance of reaching the middle class. Those are honestly great odds, and we should be proud to live in a country with such opportunity. Do those things in socialist Venezuela, and you'll still be waiting in line for your ration of bread.

QUICK-DRAW POINTS:

- Our culture should fill in the gaps in the free market that people will inevitably fall through. Not everyone will be able to avoid at least temporary poverty, and communities, churches, organizations, and private individuals should pick up this slack.

- Forcing someone to fill gaps in the economy through taxation is not moral. The person levying the tax is performing an immoral act in order to appear moral so that they can win more votes.

- The United States was founded on Judeo-Christian values and these values still hold true today as a good baseline for our culture. This does not mean that everyone needs to be religious, but we should all have some sort of common moral compass that guides our culture.

THE NEED FOR THE RIGHT CULTURE

- We should encourage personal responsibility rather than victimhood. By doing this, people will be more apt to taking matters into their own hands. This will encourage people to find new ways to succeed and may even lead them to finding a hidden talent they never knew they had. Keep encouraging victimhood, though, and people will be much less likely to find these hidden talents.

16. A CHRISTIAN PERSPECTIVE

Let me start this chapter by being very clear: This section is not intended to slight any religion, or even atheism. Nor is it intended as an argument for Christianity. This section was nearly cut from the list simply because not everyone is a Christian. Your choice of religion, or choice to not follow a religion, is your choice. This section is simply for those who have friends or family that claim Christianity as their justification for endorsing socialism or communism. Obviously, if you are a Christian, you cannot use what you believe God would want as the basis for an economic argument with an atheist, but I have listened to people have this debate and it is clear that the free-market supporters can use a bit of ammunition. Also, full disclosure: I am not a biblical scholar. These are simply my interpretations of some of Jesus's teachings, but I believe they do a good job of analyzing these teachings in a way that bolsters the arguments in this book.

A CHRISTIAN PERSPECTIVE

Some people claim that Jesus would have been a socialist because he encouraged giving the shirt from your back to the needy, among other various altruistic acts. While this is true, Jesus never forced anyone to perform such actions, and if we take a closer look at his teachings, we will find that his worldview seemed quite libertarian.

In Mark 12:17, Jesus famously says, "Give to Caesar what is Caesar's, and to God what is God's." He seems to be saying that Caesar, and everyone else for that matter, should be given what they deserve or earn. This is a very individualistic way of looking at things. Jesus did not say, "Take everything from Caesar and disperse it among everyone." Nor did he say, "Give everything you have to Caesar so that he can disperse it among everyone else." He seems to say that Caesar should be given what he earns, just like someone would in a free-market economy.

The Parable of the Talents seems to lend support to this interpretation. In this parable, Jesus describes a business owner of some kind who leaves money to his servants to watch over while he's away. The owner gives a designated amount of money to each of the servants based on their *ability*. Long story short, when the owner returns, he punishes the servant who did not create more wealth from the money (he hid his share so that it would not be lost or stolen) and rewards the ones who did. He didn't take the newfound wealth from the two productive servants and give it to the one who didn't make any.

Another common claim goes like this: *"Jesus said we should take care of the poor and give to the needy. Thus, we need to tax the rich to give to the poor."* Jesus never condoned theft. Taking from someone and giving to another person is theft, even if people vote for it. Jesus called for people to give out of the kindness of their hearts, and in secret. In Matthew 6:2, Jesus said, "When you give to the poor, don't be like the hypocrites." The hypocrites in this case were those who flaunted their giving and other virtues for all to see so that the people would praise them. Kind of like when a politician flies around on a jet proclaiming that the rich must give up their earnings in order to subsidize the poor. This isn't altruistic giving in secret, this is taking from someone because you won the vote.

Let's keep in mind that the most outspoken politician in favor of raising taxes on the wealthy owns three homes.[75] Seems like a slight double standard. You know whom I'm referring to. (But if you don't: it's a certain senator from Vermont.)

If we define theft as taking someone's private property against their will, the Ten Commandments are also pretty clear about this, as one of them clearly said not to steal. You will be hard-pressed to find someone that honestly loves to cut the government a check every year and would still send the same amount even if their tax rate shrank.

The Ten Commandments also stood against coveting your neighbor's possessions. When someone votes to tax another person because they want

A CHRISTIAN PERSPECTIVE

some of that person's wealth, they are not respecting this commandment.

Here's another common argument of those sympathetic to socialism or communism: *"But income inequality is bad. We need to make everyone equal, because it is not fair for someone to make more."* Income inequality only means that someone offered a more sought-after product than someone else. Inequality is not proof of unfairness or injustice, and Jesus seemed to agree with this. In Luke 12:13–15, a man comes to Jesus and asks him to tell the man's brother to split the family inheritance equally (the brother was set to receive more). Jesus replies, "Friend, who made me a judge over you to decide such things as that?" Even Jesus, the Son of God, said it is not his place to decide these things. Jesus went on to warn the man about the dangers of greed. By warning the man about greed, the implication was that wanting a portion of the inheritance that was not given to him was greedy.

Jesus's father was a carpenter with his own business. He was never approached by an irate Jesus, proclaiming that his support of the patriarchal institution of capitalism and his collection of profits were evil. In fact, Jesus became a self-employed carpenter himself for a time. I guess even the Son of God needs to pay the rent.

Jesus was clearly not a fan of coercion. He never forced anyone to follow him, and if we take his proclamation of being the Son of God as truth, he is probably the only person to ever have that right. Yet he never did this. He certainly encouraged people to follow him and act in a certain way, but force wasn't used. Forced "altruism" through government redistribution of wealth is not altruism.

Socialism never intended to actually help the poor. Socialism simply keeps the poor poor while pulling ever more people into poverty, thus creating a class of elites that can rule over the population and blame their suffering on capitalists. If Jesus were to choose a political ideology based off his teachings—which he never would, because it was not his purpose—he would certainly not choose an ideology that creates more suffering. If anything, he would choose capitalism simply because it is the only system where a person who came from dust can honestly ascend to the highest points of the economy.

QUICK-DRAW POINTS:

- **Jesus seemed to be quite libertarian in his thinking. He told stories of being rewarded for good tasks, even when they concerned money, and missing out on rewards for performing jobs that were considered not well done.**

- **Jesus never forced anyone to follow him. Everyone had the right to choose their own path in his mind.**

- **Even when given the opportunity to act in a communistic way—such as in the story of the inheritance in the book of Luke—Jesus did not. The only person he went after was the man asking him to act that way, and he called the man greedy for his behavior.**

17. FINAL NOTES

To the small-business owner out there that did not pay themselves for years, or had to put payroll on a credit card while their family still needed to be fed: you aren't some greedy less-than-human, and you deserve to operate your business without having government on your back. To the entrepreneur that dreams of one day beating out some of the greatest companies of today: your dreams are not rooted in evil—in fact, they are quite commendable. To the business owners who have done quite well for themselves: you *did* build that, and I know that the vast, vast majority of you care deeply for your employees. To the middle-class family that sees their purchasing power weaken every year and fears that your retirement will never materialize: you deserve to live in a society that rewards your work and does not inflate your savings into dust. I could give hundreds of different examples of ordinary citizens who are hampered by big government, but the point is that we will stop at nothing to secure your liberty once again.

The debate between capitalism and socialism or communism is really a debate between liberty and tyranny. While capitalism offers the populace liberty, socialism and communism, by definition, strip liberty from the populace. Socialism and communism do not allow you to pursue your lifelong dream of starting that company. Under capitalism, you can take that risk. You may make it big, or you may fail. But the beauty is that you can start again tomorrow.

Universities are pumping young people out who believe that the system is rigged against them. They are taught to believe that they live in a racist, sexist country that will only feed the rich white guy. If they are not paid as much as they feel entitled to be paid, or if something in their life appears to be insurmountable, they believe the blame lies with capitalism.

The problem is that the United States, due to legislative action, has slowly been marching away from capitalism. The New Deal alone would have been enough to make our Founders rebel a second time. Direct taxation was once unconstitutional, but the Sixteenth Amendment made it possible. Before it, the federal government was funded by tariffs (yes, I know, the secret tax that I criticized earlier). To assume that the Constitution will protect us from tyranny forever is to walk to the gallows. The Constitution does the best that it can to protect us, but it cannot hold the line by itself.

FINAL NOTES

Everyone can agree on the importance of the middle class. They are the people who move the economy. They buy and produce the products that make us so strong. Yet, our middle class has been shrinking for many years.[76] Leave things as they are, and we will continue to move toward a nation of a few elites and many poor people. Many years of an increase in the size of government have not created a larger middle class, yet politicians still call for an increase in the size and scope of government. This is no mistake or coincidence.

Changes toward a freer market need to be calculated carefully and implemented somewhat gently, though. When the Soviet Union fell, the people suffered greatly because the switch to capitalism came much too quickly for a purely communist society. This arguably caused Russia to end up as an oligarchy. Of course, the United States is far from what the Soviet Union was, but the principle still applies. It would be foolish to completely cut Social Security tomorrow. These things need to come in phases and, in my opinion, the market should be freed up before social programs are stopped. Doing it this way will make it so that there are more opportunities for people fully re-entering the free market.

(You may notice that the order I suggested in which to convert the economy goes against what I said in an earlier chapter, because cutting taxes before cutting social programs would bring on more debt. However, given the current circumstances in the country, I believe proceeding in this order is the better and more realistic alternative. Once a clear path toward the free market is established, we should refocus on getting rid of our debt.)

We've been blinded by the darkness of tyranny. It tells us that more government, more tyranny, is the answer. The only true answer at this point is the torch of liberty. And the only way to bring the light of liberty to the world is through action. This is easier said than done, I know. But we must stand up in our classes, workplaces, news outlets, and debates. We must expose big government for what it truly is: a power-grabbing scheme that only has ill outcomes waiting for the people.

If you do not stand for liberty, who will? The RINOs in Congress? No doubt it can be hard to get what you want in Washington. Politicians from the other side of the aisle want what they want as well. But when you are "compromising" by always giving the other side what they want and never getting anything in return, you are losing.

One of the biggest things that peeves me, and probably you if you happen to be on my side of the aisle, is when a conservative in Washington folds as soon as they are called a racist or sexist on TV. They probably do this with their next election cycle in mind, since they do not want to ruffle any feathers. But instead of digging their feet in and pointing out the fact that it is actually the policies they are fighting against that hurt minorities, they fold. Those people cannot be relied upon to secure liberty.

You already have history on your side, but now you have the ability to turn charges of racism, sexism, greed, and any other slur big-government advocates deploy on their head. They have nothing now, so what do you have to fear?

A young America technically lost the Battle of Bunker Hill during the Revolutionary War. However, it was a pyrrhic victory for the British. The British losses gave the American rebels proof that freedom was obtainable—all because some 1,500 troops were unwilling to give up even after their ammunition was depleted. When tyranny charges toward you, dig in and hold your ground. If we must fall, let us fall on the line and be resolved in facing tyranny when we do.

America has fought for freedom since its conception. We freed ourselves, and helped keep the world free, through two world wars. The war we are engaged in now is not a war of conventional arms, but one of ideology. This does not take away from its importance or potential for change, however. If tyranny wins, it will be as though the Berlin Wall never fell. If we win, the world will be free to live another day until the next generation takes our place.

If thousands of young Americans with real hopes and dreams could run into a meat grinder on a beach in Western Europe that did not even belong to them for liberty, we can charge into ideological battles with vigor for liberty as well. I know it's easiest to just let history play its course and hope that people will come around eventually, but that is no guarantee. By that point, it will have been too late. Give up now, and every painful stride made for liberty will have been in vain.

Have hope, though. There is evidence to suggest that Generation Z, America's youngest generation, is the most conservative generation since the Second World War.[77] I believe that liberty is just beginning to peak over the horizon once again. I also believe that there is a spiritual world beyond our own. We can debate, as every religion has for centuries, over what happens after we die, but I do believe that the inhabitants of that world are watching. The forces of good in the world are pulling for us and when the future looks dim and liberty appears to be on the ropes, they send in the best. That's *you*. Do not let tyranny conquer us in the end. If not for yourself, then for the next generation. I look forward to seeing you on the battlefield.

Special thanks to Mallory Stender

ENDNOTES

1. Scott Manning, "Communist Body Count," *Historian on the Warpath* (blog), December 4, 2006, http://www.scottmanning.com/content/communist-body-count/.

2. Nima Sanandaji, "The Nordic Democratic-Socialist Myth," *National Review*, July 26, 2016, http://www.nationalreview.com/article/438331/nordic-democratic-socialist-model-exposing-lefts-myth.

3. "Obama: If You've Got a Business, You Didn't Build That," YouTube (video), July 16, 2012, accessed November 1, 2017, https://www.youtube.com/watch?v=YKjPI6no5ng.

4. Greg McClure-Purude, "$15 an Hour Wages Could Nudge Fast Food Prices," Futurity.org, July 30, 2015, http://www.futurity.org/fast-food-minimum-wage-971132.

5. Nicholas Carlson, "A Google Programmer 'Blew Off' a $500,000 Salary at a Startup—Because He's Already Making $3 Million Every Year," *Business Insider*, January 10, 2014, http://www.businessinsider.com/a-google-programmer-blew-off-a-500000-salary-at-

startup-because-hes-already-making-3-million-every-year-2014-1.

6   http://www.nrn.com/people/mcdonald-s-ceo-paid-154m-2016

7   "Global 2000: Top Regard Companies: #215, McDonald's," *Forbes*, accessed November 1, 2017, https://www.forbes.com/companies/mcdonalds/.

8   "20 Billionaires Who Started with Nothing," *BloombergBusinessweek.com*, November 23, 2010, http://images.businessweek.com/slideshows/20101123/twenty-billionaires-who-started-with-nothing.

9   Cleve R. Wootson Jr., "A Dairy Queen Owner Unleashed a Racist Tirade Against a Customer. He No Longer Has a Business," *Washington Post*, January 9, 2001, https://www.washingtonpost.com/news/post-nation/wp/2017/01/09/a-dairy-queen-owner-unleashed-a-racist-tirade-against-a-customer-he-no-longer-has-a-business/.

10   Steven Perlberg, "American Median Incomes by Race Since 1967," *Business Insider*, September 17, 2013, http://www.businessinsider.com/heres-median-income-in-the-us-by-race-2013-9.

11   "Ben Shapiro Joking About 'Asian Priv[i]lege,'" YouTube (video), April 22, 2016, accessed November 1, 2017, https://www.youtube.com/watch?v=KNyfyowo-ao.

12   Steven J. Dubner, "The True Story of the Gender Pay Gap," *Freakonomics*, January 7, 2016,

http://freakonomics.com/podcast/the-true-story-of-the-gender-pay-gap-a-new-freakonomics-radio-podcast/.

13   Mark Hugo Lopez and Ana Gonzalez-Barrera, "Women's College Enrollment Gains Leave Men Behind," Pew Research Center, March 6, 2014, http://www.pewresearch.org/fact-tank/2014/03/06/wom-

ens-college-enrollment-gains-leave-men-behind/; Deborah Jones Merritt and Kyle McEntee, "The Leaky Pipeline for Women Entering the Legal Profession," Law School Transparency, *November 2016 Research Summary (report)*, https://www.lstradio.com/women/documents/MerrittAndMcEnteeResearch-Summary_Nov-2016.pdf.

14 "Women in Their 20s Earn More than Men of Same Age, Study Finds," *Guardian* (US Edition), August 28, 2015,

    https://www.theguardian.com/money/2015/aug/29/women-in-20s-earn-more-men-same-age-study-finds.

15 Peter Jacobs, "Harvard Is Being Accused of Treating Asians the Same Way It Used to Treat Jews," *Business Insider*, December 4, 2014, http://www.businessinsider.com/the-ivy-leagues-history-of-discriminating-against-jews-2014-12.

16 Jennifer Depaul, "The EPA's Lead-Paint Balloon," *Fiscal Times*, November 13, 2011, http://www.thefiscaltimes.com/Articles/2011/11/13/The-EPAs-Lead-Paint-Lead-Balloon#page1.

17 Mike McPhate, "Uber and Lyft End Rides in Austin to Protest Fingerprint Background Checks," *New York Times*, May 9, 2016, https://www.nytimes.com/2016/05/10/technology/uber-and-lyft-stop-rides-in-austin-to-protest-fingerprint-background-checks.html.

18 Teresa Oelke, "ObamaCare and Part-Time Employment: Shame on Who?" *The Hill*, March 10, 2015,

    http://thehill.com/blogs/congress-blog/economy-budget/235091-obamacare-and-part-time-employment-shame-on-who.

19 Eric Giunta, "'I Can't Expand': Florida's Small-Business Victims of Obamacare Mandate," *Sunshine State*

News, April 22, 2013, http://sunshinestatenews.com/story/i-cant-expand-floridas-small-business-victims-obamacare-mandate.

20 Sean Hackbarth, "Small Businesses Tell Congress They Can't Afford Obamacare," U.S. Chamber of Commerce (web), February 11, 2017, https://www.uschamber.com/above-the-fold/small-businesses-tell-congress-they-can-t-afford-obamacare.

21 Alicia Adamczyk, "These Are the Companies With the Best Parental Leave Policies," *Money.com*, November 4, 2015,

http://time.com/money/4098469/paid-parental-leave-google-amazon-apple-facebook/.

22 "Small Business Trends," U.S. Small Business Association, accessed August 2017, https://www.sba.gov/managing-business/running-business/energy-efficiency/sustainable-business-practices/small-business-trends.

23 William Laffer, "How Regulation Is Destroying American Jobs," Heritage Foundation *Backgrounder*, No. 96, February 16, 1993, http://www.heritage.org/government-regulation/report/how-regulation-destroying-american-jobs.

24 Kent Hoover, "10 Regulations that Give Small Business Owners the Worst Headaches," Bizjournals.com, April 28, 2016, http://www.bizjournals.com/bizjournals/washingtonbureau/2016/04/10-regulations-that-give-small-business-owners-the.html.

25 Sheila Fitzpatrick, Everyday Stalinism: Ordinary Life in Extraordinary Times: Soviet Russia in the 1930s (New York: Oxford University Press, 1999).

26 John Harwood, "10 Questions with Bernie Sanders," CNBC, May 26, 2015, http://www.cnbc.com/2015/05/26/10-questions-with-bernie-sanders.html.

ENDNOTES

27 "Soviet Cars," *History of Russia* (blog), http://historyofrussia.org/soviet-cars/.

28 Katie Pavlich, "Oh My: Bernie Sanders Thinks Bread Lines Are a Good Thing," Townhall.com, April 6, 2016, https://townhall.com/tipsheet/katiepavlich/2016/04/06/oh-my-bernie-sanders-thinks-bread-lines-are-a-good-representation-of-economic-stability-n2144137.

29 Max Farrand, "The Taxation of Tea, 1767-1773," *The American Historical Review* 3, no. 2 (1898): 266-69. doi:10.2307/1832503, https://www.jstor.org/stable/1832503?seq=1#page_scan_tab_contents.

30 Matthew Frankel, "What's the Average American's Tax Rate?" The Motley Fool, March 4, 2017, https://www.fool.com/retirement/2017/03/04/whats-the-average-americans-tax-rate.aspx.

31 John Harwood, "Bernie Sanders Questions Morality of US Economy," CNBC, May 26, 2015, https://www.cnbc.com/2015/05/26/bernie-sanders-questions-morality-of-us-economy.html.

32 Kelly Phillips Erb, "Report: Americans Spend More Than 8.9 Billion Hours Each Year On Tax Compliance," *Forbes*, June 20, 2016, https://www.forbes.com/sites/kellyphillipserb/2016/06/20/report-americans-spend-more-than-8-9-billion-hours-each-year-on-tax-compliance/#5af9afb03456.

33 "Car Ownership in U.S. Cities Map," *Governing*, http://www.governing.com/gov-data/car-ownership-numbers-of-vehicles-by-city-map.html.

34 "U-3 Unemployment Rate Was 4.5 percent in March 2017; U-6 Was 8.9 percent," Bureau of Labor Statistics, https://www.bls.gov/opub/ted/2017/u-3-unemployment-rate-was-4-point-5-percent-in-march-2017-u-6-was-8-point-9-percent.htm.

35 "Databases, Tables & Calculators by Subject," U.S.

Unemployment rate chart from 1947 to 2016, Bureau of Labor Statistics, https://data.bls.gov/timeseries/LNU04000000?years_option=all_years&periods_option=specific_periods&periods=Annual+Data.

36 Jacob Poushter, "Car, Bike or Motorcycle? Depends On Where You Live," Pew Research Center, April 16, 2015, http://www.pewresearch.org/fact-tank/2015/04/16/car-bike-or-motorcycle-depends-on-where-you-live/.

37 "The First Mobile Phone Call Was Placed 40 Years Ago Today," Fox News, April 3, 2013, http://www.foxnews.com/tech/2013/04/03/first-mobile-phone-call-was-placed-40-years-ago-today.html.

38 Monica Anderson, "Technology Device Ownership: 2015," Pew Research Center, October 29, 2015, http://www.pewinternet.org/2015/10/29/technology-device-ownership-2015/.

39 Avik Roy, "Bernie Sanders' Single-Payer Health Care Plan Would Increase Federal Spending By At Least $28 Trillion," *Forbes*, https://www.forbes.com/sites/theapothecary/2016/01/18/bernie-sanders-incredible-28-trillion-plan-to-replace-obamacare-with-single-payer-health-care/#21e8311e5bc7

40 Rafael Osío Cabrices, "Black Market Medicine and Animal Drugs: What It's Like to be Sick in Venezuela,"*HuffPost*, February 17, 2016, http://www.huffingtonpost.com/rafael-osao-cabrices/venezuela-drug-shortage_b_9154498.html.

41 Seol Song Ah, "Black Market Diagnoses Saving More Lives," *Daily NK*, September 11, 2015, http://www.dailynk.com/english/read.php?cataId=nk01500&num=13458

42 Alyene Senger, "Lack of Competition in Obamacare's Exchanges: Over Half of U.S. Has Two or Fewer Carriers," Heritage Foundation Issue Brief, No. 4082,

November 8, 2013, http://www.heritage.org/health-care-reform/report/lack-competition-obamacares-exchanges-over-half-us-has-two-or-fewer.

43 Ben Kamisar, "TSA fails internal test, lets fake bombs through," *The Hill*, June 1, 2015, http://thehill.com/business-a-lobbying/243600-tsa-fails-internal-test-lets-fake-bombs-through.

44 "Burwell v Hobby Lobby: Landmark Supreme Court Case," http://hobbylobbycase.com.

45 Nick Clements, "Obamacare Premiums Increase 25%: Is The 'Death Spiral' Here?" *Forbes*, October 25, 2016, https://www.forbes.com/sites/nickclements/2016/10/25/obamacare-premiums-increase-25-is-the-death-spiral-here/#4616291b6429.

46 "How Much of U.S. Energy Consumption and Electricity Generation Comes from Renewable Energy Sources?" U.S. Energy Information Administration, accessed November 1, 2017, https://www.eia.gov/tools/faqs/faq.php?id=92&t=4.

47 "Renewable Energy Production By State," United States Secretary of Energy, accessed November 1, 2017, https://energy.gov/maps/renewable-energy-production-state.

48 James Bushnell, "Breaking News! California Electricity Prices Are High," *Energy Institute Blog*, Energy Institute at Haas, February 21, 2017, https://energyathaas.wordpress.com/2017/02/21/breaking-news-california-electricity-prices-are-high/.

49 "Go Green, KILL PEOPLE! (Crowder Visits Mexico)," video, Louder with Crowder, accessed November 1, 2017, https://www.louderwithcrowder.com/go-green-kill-people-crowder-visits-mexico/.

50 Eric Holthaus, "Yak Dung Is Making Climate Change Worse," *Slate*, December 4, 2017, http://www.slate.com/articles/technology/future_tense/2014/12/

yak_dung_is_making_climate_change_worse_and_new_cookstoves_don_t_help.html.

51 Steve Nix, "U.S. Forest Facts on Forestland," ThoughtCo.com, April 2, 2017, https://www.thoughtco.com/us-forest-facts-on-forestland-1343034.

52 "Forest area (% of land area): Venezuela," World Bank Data Catalog, World Bank Group, accessed November 2, 2017, http://data.worldbank.org/indicator/AG.LND.FRST.ZS?locations=VE.

53 "Top Ten Countries with World's Largest Oil Reserves," *Energy Business Review*, April 21, 2017, http://explorationanddevelopment.energy-business-review.com/news/top-ten-countries-with-worlds-largest-oil-reserves-5793487.

54 Drew Johnson, "EXCLUSIVE: Al Gore's Home Devours 34 Times More Electricity than Average U.S. Household," *Daily Caller*, August 2, 2017, http://dailycaller.com/2017/08/02/exclusive-al-gores-home-devours-34-times-more-electricity-than-average-u-s-household/.

55 Michael S. Malone, "Silicon Insider: When Did Amazon Get Profitable?" ABC News, January 30,

http://abcnews.go.com/Business/story?id=87393&page=1

56 Mark J. Perry, "The Public Thinks the Average Company Makes a 36% Profit Margin, Which Is About 5X Too High," *AEIdeas* (blog), American Enterprise Institute, April 2, 2015, http://www.aei.org/publication/the-public-thinks-the-average-company-makes-a-36-profit-margin-which-is-about-5x-too-high/.

57 "Socialized Health Care: The Communist Dream and the Soviet Reality," Foundation for Economic Education, December 19, 2008, accessed November 2, 2017,

https://fee.org/resources/socialized-health-care-the-communist-dream-and-the-soviet-reality/.

58 Christopher Chantrill, "A usgovernmentspending.com Briefing: Welfare Spending," usgovernmentspending.com (blog), accessed November 2, 2017, https://www.usgovernmentspending.com/welfare_spending.

59 "Michael Jordan Quotes," BrainyQuote, accessed November 2, 2017, https://www.brainyquote.com/quotes/quotes/m/michaeljor127660.html.

60 Gordon B. Dahl, Andreas Ravndal Kostøl, Magne Mogstad, "Family Welfare Cultures," *The Quarterly Journal of Economics*, Volume 129, Issue 4, November 1 2014, Pages 1711–1752, https://doi.org/10.1093/qje/qju019.

61 Ron Haskins, "Three Simple Rules Poor Teens Should Follow to Join the Middle Class," op-ed, Brookings Institution website, March 13, 2013, https://www.brookings.edu/opinions/three-simple-rules-poor-teens-should-follow-to-join-the-middle-class/.

62 Thayer Watkins, "The Stalin Model for the Control and Coordination of Enterprises in a Socialist Economy," personal webpage, http://www.sjsu.edu/faculty/watkins/stalinmodel.htm.

63 "Close the Gaps: Disparities that Threaten America," post on Bernie Sanders's U.S. Senate page, August 5, 2011, https://www.sanders.senate.gov/newsroom/must-read/close-the-gaps-disparities-that-threaten-america.

64 Max Fisher and Amanda Taub, "How Venezuela Went from the Richest Economy in South America to the Brink of Financial Ruin," *Independent*, May 21, 2017, http://www.independent.co.uk/news/long_reads/how-venezuela-went-from-the-richest-economy-in-south-america-to-the-brink-of-financial-ruin-a7740616.html.

65 "The World's Largest Oil Reserves by Country," WorldAtlas, accessed November 2, 2017,

http://www.worldatlas.com/articles/the-world-s-largest-oil-reserves-by-country.html.

66 Emma Graham-Harrison, "Hunger Eats Away at Venezuela's Soul as Its People Struggle to Survive," *Guardian* (US edition), August 26, 2017, https://www.theguardian.com/world/2017/aug/26/nicolas-maduro-donald-trump-venezuela-hunger.

67 Tamsin Carlisle, "Venezuela Seizes 60 firms," *The National* (United Arab Emirates), May 9, 2009,

https://www.thenational.ae/business/venezuela-seizes-60-firms-1.537373.

68 Patrick Gillespie and Stefano Pozzebon, "Venezuelans Scramble for Food, But It's Often Out Of Reach," CNN Money, July 27, 2017, http://money.cnn.com/2017/07/27/news/economy/venezuela-food-shortage/index.html.

69 "Food Shortages at the Heart Of Venezuelan Economic and Political Crisis," All Things Considered, NPR, May 21, 2017, http://www.npr.org/2017/05/21/529419484/food-shortages-at-the-heart-of-venezuelan-economic-and-political-crisis.

70 Prableen Bajpai, "North Korean vs. South Korean Economies," Investopedia, April 5, 2015, http://www.investopedia.com/articles/forex/040515/north-korean-vs-south-korean-economies.asp.

71 Katherine Lam, "North Korea's Kim Keeps Teen Sex Slaves, Executes Musicians with Anti-Aircraft Guns, Defector Reveals," Fox News, September 20, 2017, http://www.foxnews.com/world/2017/09/20/kim-jong-un-plucks-teen-sex-slaves-from-schools-north-korean-defector-reveals.html.

ENDNOTES

72 Dan Reiter, "Democratic Peace Theory," Oxford Bibliographies, last modified September 27, 2017, http://www.oxfordbibliographies.com/view/document/obo-9780199756223/obo-9780199756223-0014.xml.

73 Jonathan Haidt, The Righteous Mind: Why Good People Are Divided by Politics and Religion (New York: Pantheon, 2012).

74 "The Almanac of American Philanthropy: Statistics," Philanthropy Roundtable, accessed November 2, 2017, http://www.philanthropyroundtable.org/almanac/statistics/.

75 Tina Nguyen, "Bernie Sanders Buys His Third House," *Vanity Fair*, August 9, 2016, https://www.vanityfair.com/news/2016/08/bernie-sanders-summer-house.

76 "A Portrait of America's Middle Class, by the Numbers," NPR, July 7, 2016, http://www.npr.org/2016/07/07/484941939/a-portrait-of-americas-middle-class-by-the-numbers.

77 Salena Zito, "Why the Generation After Millennials Will Vote Republican," *New York Post*, July 1, 2017, http://nypost.com/2017/07/01/why-the-next-generation-after-millennials-will-vote-republican/.

CPSIA information can be obtained
at www.ICGtesting.com
Printed in the USA
FSOW02n1530141217
42136FS